Jaws of Death:
Gate of Heaven

WORKS BY DIETRICH VON HILDEBRAND

IN ENGLISH
Liturgy and Personality†
Transformation in Christ†
Jaws of Death: Gate of Heaven†
Marriage: The Mystery of Faithful Love†
In Defense of Purity
Fundamental Moral Attitudes
Ethics
The New Tower of Babel
Situation Ethics
Graven Images
What is Philosophy?
Not as the World Gives
Man and Woman
The Heart
The Trojan Horse in the City of God
The Devastated Vineyard
Celibacy and the Crisis of Faith
The Encyclical *Humanae Vitae*
Satan at Work

IN GERMAN
Die Idee der sittlichen Handlung
Sittlichkeit und ethische Werterkenntnis
Metaphysik der Gemeinschaft
Das katholische Berufsethos
Engelbert Dollfuss: Ein katholischer Staatsmann
Zeitliches im Lichte des Ewigen
Der Sinn philosophischen Fragens und Erkennens
Die Menschheit am Scheideweg
Mozart, Beethoven, Schubert
Heiligkeit und Tüchtigkeit
Das Wesen der Liebe
Die Dankbarkeit
Ästhetik I & II
Moralia

†Available from Sophia Institute Press

Dietrich von Hildebrand

Jaws of Death: Gate of Heaven

SOPHIA INSTITUTE PRESS
Manchester, New Hampshire

Jaws of Death: Gate of Heaven was first published in German in 1980 as *Über den Tod*. This first English translation of *Über den Tod* is published by Sophia Institute with the permission of Alice von Hildebrand.

German-language edition Copyright © 1980 Alice von Hildebrand
English translation Copyright © 1991 Alice von Hildebrand
Printed in the United States of America
All rights reserved
Jacket by Joan M. Barger

Sophia Institute Press
Box 5284, Manchester, NH 03108
1-800-888-9344

Library of Congress Cataloging-in-Publication Data

Von Hildebrand, Dietrich, 1889-1977
    [Über den Tod. English]
    Jaws of death, gate of heaven / Dietrich von Hildebrand.
      p. cm.
    Translation of: Über den Tod.
    Includes bibliographical references.
    ISBN 0-918477-10-7 Cloth : $14.95
    1. Death—Religious aspects—Christianity. 2. Death. I. Title.
BT825.V5813   1990   236'.1—dc20   90-46365
                                               CIP

10 9 8 7 6 5 4 3

CONTENTS

Foreword

by Alice von Hildebrand, Ph.D.

EIGHTY-SIX years old and conscious of the near approach of his own death, my husband, Dietrich von Hildebrand, wrote this book in just two weeks. Although written quickly, it is nonetheless the fruit of years of thought and prayer during which my husband repeatedly confronted the prospect of his own death.

He had survived a severe heart attack in 1964, but for years thereafter continued to suffer from a serious heart condition. Time and again he had close calls with death. By 1976 he was eighty-six years old and his strength was waning. He told me: "I have been battling against death for years; I wanted to remain with you, but now I must face the fact that I am losing the fight. It is time for me to face death, and I have accepted it."

This book is the fruit of his mature acceptance of death, which he had come to see in the light of eternity. In writing these pages, however, my husband did not minimize death's horror or downplay its significance. He never lost that reverent fear of death and of God's judgment which is reflected so well in the *Dies Irae* (previously sung at Catholic funerals):

Jaws of Death: Gate of Heaven

Dies irae, dies illa,
Solvet saeclum in favilla,
Teste David cum Sibylla.

Quantus tremor est futurus,
Quando judex est venturus,
Cuncta stricte discussurus!

Tuba mirum spargens sonum
Per sepulchra regionum,
Coget omnes ante thronum.

Mors stupebit et natura,
Cum resurget creatura,
Judicanti responsura.[1]

Dreaded day, that day of ire,
When the world shall melt in fire,
Told by Sibyl and David's lyre.

Fright mens' hearts shall rudely shift,
As the Judge through gleaming rift
Comes each soul to closely sift.

Then, the trumpet's shrill refrain,
Piercing tombs by hill and plain,
Souls to judgment shall arraign.

---

[1] *Dies Irae*, stanzas 1-4, Sequence of the *Requiem Mass* attributed to Thomas of Celano.

Death and nature stand aghast,
As the bodies rising fast,
Hie to hear the sentence passed.

It is true, of course, that despite these fearful aspects of death, many Christian mystics and privileged saints have longed for death. Dietrich von Hildebrand knew this well, but he also knew that before reaching this pinnacle, they had gone through many stages of profound spiritual growth. He was wary of those who, with false simplicity, jump to the conclusion that death is marvelous because it implies an encounter with our Creator.

Unfortunately, even among believing Christians, a strong tendency to downplay the fearfulness of death has developed since Vatican II. Compare the above-quoted lines with our contemporary Liturgy which celebrates death almost as if it guarantees an immediate entrance into eternal beatitude. The *Alleluia* is sung and the atmosphere is sometimes almost festive, with the bereaved confidently and joyfully telling others that their beloved is now surely free from all suffering.

In fact, we have no absolute certainty that the deceased is already enjoying eternal beatitude; and it is quite reasonable to assume that very many of us will have to pass through the purifying fires of Purgatory. There our sufferings will be dreadful as our illusions about ourselves are stripped from us. Facing God in His justice and majesty, we will be made acutely aware of our own sinfulness and our need for His mercy.

Dietrich von Hildebrand was keenly aware of this. He also knew that death came into the world as a punishment for sin. Therefore, in the first half of this book, he reveals its mystery and horror. He shows why *we should fear death*. It is *meant* to awaken fear in us, and does so in all but the most spiritually obtuse.

Jaws of Death: Gate of Heaven

Death's promise

My husband's dark beginning to this book renders its second half all the more luminous and radiant. While confronting the full horror of death, he remained an ardent believer and knew that Christ, our Savior, has conquered death and its horror. With St. Paul, Dietrich von Hildebrand demands, "O death, where is thy victory? O death, where is thy sting?"[2]

He devotes the second half of this book to death viewed in the light of the Redemption. These latter pages are permeated by hope, by the anticipated joy that one day we shall meet God directly; we shall see the sweet face of Christ; we shall contemplate His Holy Mother and the army of saints in Heaven.

Unlike most recent books about death, JAWS OF DEATH: GATE OF HEAVEN faithfully presents both faces of death — its grim horror *and* its potential for infinite light and joy. Dietrich von Hildebrand shows that although death never loses its character as a punishment for sin, its fearful darkness can be pierced by the radiant light of faith — faith in God, in eternal life, in the resurrection of the body, and in the certainty of reunion with our beloved dead — a reunion that will know no sunset.

Because the jaws of death can be our gate to Heaven, the radiant aspect of death finally triumphs as the light of Christ dissipates the fearful dark clouds spread by death.

Dietrich von Hildebrand's own meeting with death

Dietrich von Hildebrand was never an "ivory-tower thinker" so absorbed in intellectual concepts and the writing of books

---

[2] 1 Cor. 15:55.

that he failed to relate his insights to his personal life. As he wrote these pages, he knew that his own death was not far off. It drew close, and I saw him face it with the humble faith that permeated his whole life and that radiates from the pages of this book.

He was hospitalized for a few weeks at the very end of September, 1976. Returning home, he continued to work on his book on aesthetics, but his breathing became more labored and I lived in a constant state of dread.

We celebrated Christmas together, but during the night of December 31st, he suffered excruciating cardiac pains. He had already received the Last Rites of the Church five times and now had to be hospitalized yet again.

My husband's condition stabilized until January 8th, when he suffered a radical drop of blood pressure and lost consciousness. He did not respond when the nurse called him by name, but when I called him, he opened his eyes.

Fr. Bradley and several friends came to his bedside to recite the prayers for the dying. With a whisper of a voice, my husband asked Fr. Bradley to pray a *Te Deum* for all the graces and blessings he had received in his life. When Fr. Bradley came to the words, *"non confundar in aeternum"* ("let me never be confounded"), my husband tried to intone the *Te Deum* of Bruckner (which he loved so much), but his voice failed him. In subsequent days, he seemed to improve somewhat. He was discharged on Monday, January 24th, but it was clear to me that the end was near.

Dietrich von Hildebrand received Holy Communion for the last time on Tuesday, January 25th. I shall never forget the ardor with which he recited the *Anima Christi,* that prayer he loved so deeply. With an intensity of faith that sprang from the very core of his ardent soul, he repeated three times to Christ the words, *"Jube me venire ad te!"* — "Bid me come to Thee!" These were practically his last words — he who had spoken so often and so beautifully about eternal life.

My husband had a very restless night. Then, early Wednesday morning, he asked for a drink of water. After receiving it, he fell back on his pillow. Dietrich von Hildebrand was about to taste the waters of eternal life.

Author's Preface

IN various works I have emphasized the crucial significance of awakenedness. Its essential importance stands out clearly when we realize that *to be awakened* (i.e., *fully conscious*) is an essential feature of personal being and even the fulfillment of personhood.

We can say that the more awakened a person is, the more his personhood is actualized. The more awakened a person is, the more he is a *self* (in the Kierkegaardian sense of the term). The more awakened he is, the more he is an individual independent of the mentality of the masses. Simultaneously, this very individuality enables him to enter into communion with other persons and to escape a dull wandering through life.

The more awakened he is, the deeper will be his grasp of values and his response to them, and the livelier will be the voice of his conscience when faced with a moral choice. The more awakened he is, the freer will he be from self-illusions and therefore from value-blindness.

This book does not examine *awakenedness* in all its dimensions, but only in relation to death.

What are the various aspects of death?

Which, if any, is the true and valid aspect?

What should be our response to the certain knowledge that we must someday die?

The decisive, mysterious event called death will become a reality for each of us. The fact is certain — only the date is veiled. I mean to discuss certain key implications of this fact.

This small book can make no claim to comprehensiveness. Not every aspect of death will be analyzed, whether natural or supernatural. On the natural level, only the centrally classic view of death will be discussed. On the supernatural, only two main Christian views will be treated.

This entire work has a very personal and existential character: I am an old man and have been directly confronted with death on several occasions. From such subjective experiences I have sought to draw out truths which are objectively true and thus valid for all men.

I shall begin with the radical difference between the natural and the supernatural view of death. I shall then treat the presuppositions which can make possible the victorious journey from the natural to the supernatural aspect.

Part I

The Natural Aspect of Death

Ways to comprehend death

LET us first consider the natural aspect of death: its complete awfulness and horror. When we consider the phenomenon of death on the purely natural plane, we see it not only as a frightful misfortune but also as a paradoxical, puzzling breaking-off of life which, in a certain respect, makes everything about life seem pointless.

The horror of death

If we focus solely on this aspect in a consistent way, we arrive at the pessimism of the great Italian poet Leopardi, for whom *death is truth:* a truth from which can be inferred "the infinite vanity of everything."[3] This metaphysical error, a consequence of Leopardi's lack of understanding of the Christian view of death, nevertheless highlights a deep truth of its own: the

---

[3] Giacomo Leopardi, *Canto 28: A se stesso,* line 16.

inadequacy of earthly life. Men continue to ask why we must die. Why must our lives be broken off so cruelly?

A woman told me how she once found her six-year-old child dissolved in tears. She asked, "Why are you crying?" Her child replied: "Because one day we must die!" The little child had indeed grasped a key aspect of death even though, at his young age, he probably had little acquaintance with the explicit teaching of both the Old and the New Testaments which characterize death as a *punishment*.

The inadequacy of life

We must see, however, that the unlimited continuation of our earthly existence would also be something unimaginable and indeed dreadful. Even though, according to our natural point of view, death is a misfortune dreaded even by many who have nothing more to expect of life, the prospect of an endless earthly life would also be fearful.

In a lecture given at the University of Munich in 1951, the late Jean Cardinal Daniélou very properly pointed out that human beings, even though they are more and more able to dominate nature, can never escape from "the cage of death." Even so, he added, if we managed to prolong earthly life indefinitely so as to do away with death, the result would be a kind of Hell, and not a blessed eternity.

Ways to comprehend death

The phenomenon of death confronts us most powerfully in two fundamentally different ways: first, through the death of someone we love deeply; and second, through thinking about our own death — that future event which inevitably comes closer every moment of our lives. These two ways of encountering death have much in common, but there are also quite different elements unique to each.

The death of someone who is not close to us

To be sure, the phenomenon of death is always present to us whenever anyone we know dies, whether they are well known by us or not, deeply beloved by us or not. Why, then, do I begin my investigations with the death of a beloved person, a *thou* who once occupied a unique place in my affections?

The death of someone who is *not* close to me is divorced from my everyday life, with its own routine and inner laws. Of course, I notice such a death, but its fearful breath does not directly affect my own world. I am not personally confronted by it; it does not reveal its secret meaning in my own life.

Certainly the reality and horror of death can also touch me if I witness an accident and see before me the broken and bleeding body of a human being. The same is true if I go through a great catastrophe such as a severe natural disaster or a deadly military battle. But in these cases, death impresses me more as a deeply sad and troubling aspect of life on earth than as the personal mystery of that sudden, radical separation from a human being I have known and loved — with all the multiformity of horror that this separation brings with it.

The death of someone I love deeply

I encounter the phenomenon of death in a complete, existential way only in the death of someone I love deeply, someone I love in an ultimate way, someone precious beyond all other humans.

To understand better the death of such a beloved human, let us first meditate on my love for such a person. Let us start with the blissful fullness of existence I experience in my loving contact with this individual human, loved above all others.

There is here the unprecedented gift of a person who most deeply corresponds to the yearnings of my heart, a person who loves me, who returns love for love. I meditate now on the total reality possessed by this beloved person — how emphatically she is *here*, in the center of my life — how much the full reality of her existence is with me.

And then she dies.

Her eyes are closed, motionless. She has ceased to speak. Communication with her has become completely impossible. She cannot hear my voice, nor can I gaze into her eyes or strain to hear her voice. Her body is cold. The very hands that once responded to my touch are lifeless. Her body is then committed to the earth, and I am surrounded by a dreadful emptiness, an unspeakable desolation. I bid a tearful, tragic farewell to the one who was the joy of my heart, the sunshine of my existence. And then I see how everyday life goes on in its dullness, seemingly as if nothing had happened.

What a contrast between my personal, dreadful loss and the drab monotony of routine life! I am faced with the end of the temporal life of the one who was the greatest source of my earthly happiness, the supreme treasure of my heart. She is dead, but everything else goes on as usual. Things which in comparison to her are quite valueless continue in existence: the clothes she once wore, the empty bed, the traffic in the street outside, the weather, the practical things of everyday life. All these have survived, but she is dead!

How absurd it all seems. What a strange contrast in the world of values! How fearful and dreadful is death that it should suddenly leave empty the place once filled by the person I loved most in all the world. How unbearable that I must now say "she was" instead of "she is"!

My beloved's death raises questions about immortality

It is true enough that, in such a case, my love can look beyond death and somehow know that my beloved cannot really die. Gabriel Marcel's words express this deep sentiment. To that unique individual for whom I feel the ultimate kind of love, I cry out, "You shall not die!"[4]

This points to everything that touches on the immortality of the soul, everything that asserts the impossibility of my loved one's merely fading away even though her body has ceased to live. Many things indeed point to immortality and, once the existence of God is admitted, even give proof of it. This indication is nowhere so pronounced — nowhere so strong and vibrant — as in the ultimate love I feel for my precious beloved. It is, in fact, my own strong love which cries out, "You shall not die!"

But even this awareness of immortality does not remove the dread of death, does not neutralize its sting. The frightfulness of separation remains; an empty loneliness gapes at me. The body and soul of my beloved had been presented to me united in a single living form. Every contact of human souls must include also their respective bodies. I have been face to face with my beloved, have gazed upon her countenance. I have recognized her; I have read from her face expressions of joy and love, and

---

[4] "To love someone means saying to him: 'You shall not die.' " ("*Aimer un être, c'est lui dire: 'Toi, tu ne mourras pas.' *") Gabriel Marcel, *Le Mort de Demain*, act 2, sc. 6, in his *Trois Pièces* (Paris: Plon, 1931), 161.

sometimes of sorrow and concern. She has been for me a single image, a blissful unity.

How can I now imagine her soul existing independently of her body? I know indeed that the physiological processes are essentially different from those of the soul. I even accept the many clear hints of immortality and thus am convinced of the continued existence of my beloved's soul. But I yet must stare at the brutal event of her body's dissolution; I am faced with the fundamental difference between her living body and her lifeless corpse.

Even if on the natural plane I am convinced that her soul has not ceased to exist, I nonetheless am constrained to ask, "Where is she?" She had in former times stood before me. I could see her dear face, her lovely form. I was able to speak to her and she was able to reply to my questions and to respond to the expression of my love. She could surprise me in her answers; her words could go far beyond anything I had expected in the way of love.

Now everything is quiet. I can no longer reach her. A frightful emptiness surrounds me. Everything I encounter impresses me with the contrast between visible, earthly reality and the puzzling absence of the one I love. I have lost the one human person loved by me without measure or comparison. I am caught up now in the tedium of life. I am filled with disgust and emptiness over the rhythm of everyday life that goes on relentlessly — as though nothing had changed, as though I had not lost my precious beloved!

The death of my beloved is the greatest of sorrows

Compared to the death of my beloved, what are all other evils and sufferings of life? This vale of tears certainly has for us a vast number and variety of sorrows — from loss of sight and the serious pains that rack our body to imprisonment in a concentration camp and the dreadful sufferings entailed by such a fate. But the loss of a beloved person follows a different course. It does not involve bodily sufferings, nor the loss of the obviously good things of life. No, the death of my beloved concerns an incredibly blissful, purely positive treasure. It marks the end of a natural spring of joy.

We touch here upon the sinister fate of all human beings: *death*, which hangs like the sword of Damocles over every human life. Each of us lives *in umbra mortis*, in the dread shadow of death. Compared to the death of someone I love, all other sufferings are merely incidental. Death threatens each of us essentially; no one is exempt. I am constantly aware that my beloved comes closer to death with each passing day. I know that death may snatch her away tomorrow.

Someone who has never known an ultimate love in this life, who has never given his heart to another human who has loved him in return, knows nothing of the fundamental horror with which the death of a beloved person surrounds us.

Now lifeless in shape is my loved one's body, which had been always included in my love (even in that non-marital form of love in which the *intention of union* does not aim at corporal union). Her body which formerly was filled with the nobility of her precious personality is now subject to a dreadful kind of decay and decomposition. Her soul has vanished into an unattainable distance and is radically cut off from us. My incomprehensible, puzzling dread of death remains in its natural aspect despite my conviction that her soul continues to exist.

St. Augustine speaks in a unique way in his *Confessions* of the night of suffering into which he was plunged by the death of his friend: "At this grief, my heart was utterly darkened; and whatever I beheld was death. My native country was a torment to me, and my father's house a strange unhappiness; and whatever I had shared with him, wanting him, became a distracting torture. Mine eyes sought him everywhere, but he was not granted them; and I hated all places, for that they had not him; nor could they now tell me, 'he is coming,' as when he was alive and absent. I became a great riddle to myself, and I asked my soul why she was so sad and why she disquieted me sorely: but she knew not what to answer me."[5]

Seeing death as a happy liberation from the prison of the body (an idea which Socrates defends[6]) makes sense only for my own death, but never for the death of a dearly beloved person. When I mentally anticipate my own death *ante mortem* — before my death — I do not experience that bewildering loneliness, that heart-breaking contrast between the unimportant things that go on living and the bleak present, now that the light of my beloved has ceased to shine.

In the case of my own death, love retreats entirely into the background. But the death of my beloved overwhelms me *post mortem* — after her death. The joy I once knew in her living presence is replaced by the horror of separation, by the dread of death as the great enemy of love and human happiness.

Only faith affords consolation when my beloved dies

For a person who loves deeply but knows only death's natural aspect, even one day's happiness is incomprehensible and, in

---

[5] St. Augustine, *Confessions*, trans. Marcus Dods, in vol. 18 of *The Great Books of the Western World* (Chicago: Encyclopedia Britannica, 1952), 4.4.

[6] Plato, *Phaedo*, 63E-69E.

fact, impossible if he has only a rational belief in the soul's immortality to oppose to the frightful character of death. Only faith in God, in Christ, and in Christian Revelation can confront this natural viewpoint in a victorious way. The *Preface* for the *Requiem Mass* of the Tridentine Liturgy admirably states: "In the same Christ the hope of a blessed resurrection has dawned for us, bringing all who are under the certain, sad sentence of death the consoling promise of future immortality."[7]

Even this faith, of course, is only a solace, a consolation: it does not take away the fearfulness of death. To be sure, the sting of death is removed — but death is not thereby stripped of its character as a punishment. For all the promises of immortality, it yet remains a great misfortune to someone whom we deeply love and, less dramatically, to anyone we love in any way.

With profundity, Novalis writes about Christ:

> Without you what would I have been?
> What without you might I be?
> A prey to fear and dread and sin,
> I'd stand alone and nothing see.
> For me no love would be secure,
> The future but a dark abyss.
> And if my sad heart could not endure,
> To whom would I go? Whence my bliss?[8]

---

[7] "*Ut, quos contristat certa moriendi conditio, eosdem consoletur futurae immortalitatis promissio.*"

[8] "*Was wär ich ohne dich gewesen?/ Was würd ich ohne dich nicht sein?/ Zu Furcht und Ängsten auserlesen,/ Ständ ich in weiter Welt allein./ Nichts wüßt ich sicher, was ich liebte,/ Die Zukunft wär ein dunkler Schlund;/ Und wenn mein Herz sich tief betrübte,/ Wem tät ich meine Sorge kund?*" Novalis, *Werke und Briefe*, "*Geistliche Lieder*," 1 (Leipzig: Insel Verlag, 1942).

The death of a dearly beloved person will once again be our theme when we view it, later on, from the supernatural standpoint expressed in the words: "Behold, the Bridegroom cometh! Go forth to meet Him!"[9]

Fear of death may not lead to understanding of it

We all know, of course, that someday we shall die. But not many of us focus on this fact day after day. The majority of people are not very conscious of their inevitable death so long as they are in good health and so long as they are spared acute anxiety over certain medical symptoms which might indicate a fatal illness.

Any of us, of course, may have a heightened awareness of death when we find ourselves in great danger (during an air raid, for example, or as soldiers in battle, passengers on a sinking ship, or victims of a serious accident). But our awareness here is more concerned with the *danger* of death: its dominant characteristic is an instinctive fear of the danger as well as an instinctive strenuous effort to save ourselves, which often takes on a frankly animalistic aspect. In other words, this does not necessarily involve a completely conscious understanding of the phenomenon of death or lead us to a contemplative confrontation with it.

Some men remain ever conscious of death

There are, however, a few persons whose lives are pervaded by the consciousness that one day they will have to die. It is also

---

[9] Mt. 25:6.

true that in times of great danger to their lives — especially when they understand that they cannot escape death through their own efforts — a good number of men will confront death with sentiments of profound composure and look it directly in the eye.

Since we are now discussing the authentically natural aspect of death, we must pay particular attention to its meaning for those who live in genuine awareness of death. We must distinguish, in this respect, those who understand death's relentless approach toward each of us from those who are alert to death because of an actually imminent danger of death rooted in a given situation.

Our metaphysical situation — as pilgrims in time with an all-too-mortal body — is the basis for our consciousness that we shall have to die at some future time (and, normally, at a certain age). It is the basis also of our consciousness that at any moment death may claim us and carry us off, whatever our expectations. Thus "in the midst of life we are surrounded by death,"[10] and we sit "in the shadow of death."[11] In these two expressions the entire dreadful quality of death confronts us.

[10] Eleventh-century response or antiphon: *"Media in vita mortis sumus."*
[11] Lk. 1:79.

II

Separation from the world we know
— death's first natural aspect

DEATH is the end of everything known to us and trusted by us, the end of every hold we have on the great pleasures of life. All the beautiful things that we are now able to see and to hear — we shall see and hear no longer. More dreadful still, all contact is broken off with persons we love. We are faced with total isolation. As Goethe says in his *Egmont*, death brings to an end "the sweet, pleasant habitude of existence."[12]

Death stands before us as a descent into nothingness. These hands of mine which now are able to grasp so many things, these hands through which I am able to accomplish so much, shall become lifeless. Their warmth will disappear. My body, in

---

[12] "*Süßes Leben! Schöne, freundliche Gewohnheit des Daseins und Wirkens! Von dir soll ich scheiden!*" ("Sweet life! Sweet pleasant habitude of existence and activity! From thee must I part!") Johann von Goethe, *Egmont*, near the end of act 5. *The Works of J. W. von Goethe*, trans. Nathan Haskell Dole (Boston: Wyman-Fogg Company, 1902), 311.

which I feel myself so much at home, will become stiff, lifeless, cold. It will decay, decompose, and stink.

Love, goodness, and beauty promise us immortality

Quite opposed to these thoughts, of course, are all those hints that support our conviction about the immortality of the soul. All true values, all realities which shine with beauty, goodness, and lovableness — all these contain the promise of a life beyond, of a fulfillment. They somehow assure us that in that deep, central event of death, we shall discover our association with eternity.

I cited earlier the beautiful words of Gabriel Marcel in which we say to our beloved: "You shall not die!" In an analogous way these same words are valid also for ourselves. When I love another, a hint of eternity shines forth; and this eternity exists for myself, too. The preciousness of my beloved, the objective glow shining forth from things good and things beautiful — these in their deepest meaning point beyond dying to a life of unlimited continuance. If death — my own or that of a beloved person — were only a descent into nothingness, a cessation of the soul's existence, the world would be a unique and dreadful absurdity. The deep promises contained in love, goodness, and beauty would be a lie.[13] Earthly life would indeed be "a tale told by an idiot, full of sound and fury, signifying nothing."[14]

The existence of an all-good God is simply irreconcilable with such an ultimate disappointment and cosmic absurdity. The fact that deep values do not mock us with false hints and

---

[13] Cf. Dietrich von Hildebrand, *Ethics* (Chicago: Franciscan Herald Press, 1972), Chaps. 13 and 15.

[14] Shakespeare, *Macbeth*, act 5, sc. 5, lines 26-28.

lying promises is guaranteed precisely by the existence of God. And yet, on the natural plane, we can know of the existence of God only "through a glass, darkly."[15] Only with great effort and rare encouragement can the natural reason of man reach the awesome, hidden, and most mysterious God whose loving Providence directs the world.[16]

Yet death remains a terrible unknown

Notwithstanding all these hints of immortality, on the natural plane death remains a dark, dreadful doorway. We are unable to imagine the *how* and the *where* of the soul that continues to exist when the body dies. We are faced with the total, radical fading away of the entire earthly reality known to us. We stare at an absolute darkness. Such considerations prevent our natural conviction about immortality from removing the dread we feel for death. Everything we see about the death of other humans, everything we contemplate concerning our own death, cannot but make us fearful before this unknown terror.

---

[15] 1 Cor. 13:12.

[16] "My immortality is necessary if only because God will not be guilty of injustice and extinguish altogether the flame of love for Him once enkindled in my heart. And what is more precious than love? Love is higher than existence, love is the crown of existence; and how is it possible that existence should not be under its dominance? If I have once loved Him and rejoiced in my love, is it possible that He should extinguish me and my joy and bring me to nothingness again? If there is a God, then I am immortal. *Voilà ma profession de foi.*" Fyodor Dostoyevsky, *The Possessed*, trans. Constance Garnett (New York: Macmillan, 1931), 623.

III

Natural evidence for immortality

SOCRATES met his death with peace and cheerfulness of soul. How was this possible? Did the dreadful aspect of death totally retreat before his great confidence in the immortality of his soul? We know that for him death represented the beginning of a higher, happier life because death frees the soul from the prison of the body. Was Socrates right thus to put away all fear of death? Some men think that death means descent into absolute nothingness. Therefore, they argue, death need not be feared because it will bring about the end of all suffering. This is a deceptive and false argument that gains plausibility from the tacitly-held concept that only a consciously-felt suffering is an evil.

Death as nonexistence is an evil

In truth, however, existence as a personal being is a great good, the basis for all other things: our happiness and bliss, our loves and yearnings. But this personal existence is so basic, so taken for granted, that we are usually not completely aware of its remarkable value.[17] If, then, we were to lose this fundamental good and descend into nothingness, this would constitute a terrible loss, a dreadful misfortune. Our no longer being able to suffer when we cease to exist would in no way mitigate the dreadful loss of personal existence.

The view that death means the fading away of our personal being is closely connected with the modern sense of the meaninglessness of life on earth. If our personal existence, so unmistakably linked to a higher fulfillment in the world beyond, were destined to be dissolved into nothingness, then our life would be a complete illusion. If the hints and promises of all great blessings were cruelly deceptive, the world would be a stage of absurdity. Only mockery and cynicism would be an appropriate response.

Now the existence of an infinitely loving, personal God excludes the possibility of such deception and consequent absurdity. The assumption, therefore, that a person's death is the total end of his unique existence is in total contradiction to our certainty that God exists. If we accept this assumption, we become, simply, atheists. The view of life which stamps it as meaningless and deceptive will have won. What further need then to speak about hopes or fears? All is absurdity.

Given the great, basic value of personal existence, it should be clear how erroneous is the argument that "death cannot be an evil if I cease to exist through it, so I need not fear it." This

---

[17] St. Augustine expresses this truth in a special way: "But as the sentient nature, even when it feels pain, is superior to the stony, which can feel none, so the rational nature, even when wretched, is more excellent than that which lacks reason or feeling, and can therefore experience no misery." *The City of God*, 12.1, trans. Marcus Dods, in vol. 18 of *The Great Books of the Western World* (Chicago: Encyclopedia Britannica, 1952).

argument, which seems deeply enlightened, is false and misleading, based as it is on a fundamental blindness to the great value of personal existence.

Death as non-personal existence is an evil

A similar argument, more and more frequently encountered today, holds that death means the end of our individual existence, but that we do continue as part of a *universal consciousness*. However, being a person and being an individual are so inseparable that the concept of a *universal consciousness* is nonsensical: it is a contradiction in terms to hold that individual persons dissolve into one grand universal consciousness that somehow continues them in being. Drops of water may indeed join together to form a lake. But persons either exist as unique individuals or they disappear. They cannot be "merged" into a "higher whole."

Every form of pantheism shares this error of interpreting death as a radical fading away of the individual person. When the conscious existence of a person as a particular individual ceases, this necessarily means the fading away of that person into nothingness.[18]

---

[18] As Kierkegaard correctly understood, every form of pantheism within the various religions is in direct contradiction to Christian Revelation. Consider, for example, his journal entry for August 20, 1838: "The 'lonely man': in this category stands and falls the cause of Christendom, after the development of the world has gone so far in reflection as it has today. Without this category, pantheism has had an absolute victory...but the category of the 'lonely man' is and remains the solid point which has been able to offer resistance to pantheistic confusion." *The Journals of Sören Kierkegaard: A Selection*, ed. and trans. Alexander Dru (London and New York: Oxford University Press, 1938; reprint 1959), 63.

Personal existence is a prerequisite for happiness

Our existence as a person is a unique blessing and an essential precondition for all happiness. To lose our personal existence would be a loss of the greatest magnitude even if it did prevent us from suffering. Suffering is a misfortune, but the objective loss of our personal being is a dreadful evil. If, in fact, death actually meant the termination of our personal existence, then death itself would be most fearful. We should then dread the ultimate annihilation of ourselves, our person, the very "I" behind every drama of our earthly life.

Socrates argues that death cannot be a misfortune if it means the fading away of personal existence into nothingness, since we would then no longer be subject to suffering. His argument is really more or less a rhetorical one, a premise assumed for the sake of argument but not really believed. For Socrates is firmly convinced of the continued existence of the individual soul, as the entire tenor of his splendid discourse on death clearly shows.

Socrates' attitude on death, which views it as a liberation, is all the more surprising when we consider how vividly strong for the Greeks was the fear of death. Their proverb claims that "it is better to be a beggar on earth than a king in the underworld." Chesterton notes that the cheerfulness and merriment of Hellas is centered on our earthly life, and that it gives way to an increasingly frightened anxiety when the question of man's fate after death is raised. In this respect it contrasts greatly with the Christian view of both earthly life and temporal death.[19]

---

[19] "The pagan was (in the main) happier and happier as he approached the earth, but sadder and sadder as he approached the heavens." G.K. Chesterton, *Orthodoxy* (New York: Doubleday Image, 1959), 158.

Socrates saw in death a great positive value — of *liberation*. In stark contrast is Dostoyevsky's description of his own state of mind when he, along with many others, was condemned to death by the Czarist government.[20] He details the frightful hours he endured as seemingly-imminent death approached — right up until the sudden and unexpected commutation of his death sentence to banishment in Siberia. Death had confronted him in all its horror. He somehow was able to find words to depict the dreadful and mysterious force that had threatened to destroy his young life at a single blow.

Certainty of immortality may not diminish fear of death

Given that we can grasp with absolute certainty that a personal, infinitely kind God exists, is not the dread of death removed? Our conviction about the infinitely good God must also prove that we are deceived by no lying "promises" about a happy life in some future existence. Is not God's existence sufficient to dispel any dread of death as being the end of our personal being?

We are faced with two views. On the one hand, death is seen as the end of everything. On the other, we are certain of our soul's immortality, for we know that God exists and we have gathered into our mind the many hints and promises — *the intimations* — of our continued existence. How shall we relate the one view with the other?

---

[20] Fyodor Dostoyevsky, *Gesammelte Briefe, 1833-1881,* tr. Friedrich Hitzer (Munich: Piper, 1966): unabbreviated letter to Michael Michaelovitch Dostoyevsky of Dec. 22, 1849, 76-81; Karl Nötzel, *Das Leben Dostojewskis* (Leipzig: Haessel-Verlag, 1925), pt. 1, II, d and e, 253-62.

If we stick to rational evidence alone, then the fearful aspect of death as the slayer of all things (including, above all, our personal consciousness) ought to modify considerably our certainty about the *intimations of immortality*. For these might just be mere impressions, whereas death is absolutely certain.

If a mere impression conflicts with a conviction rooted in absolutely certain knowledge, the latter must be decisive. Will not the scales then tip in favor of the gloom threatened by certain death? But something more than abstract insight is at stake here: our "existential" experience of all the hints about life beyond death, hints which pervade all the great and deep moments of our earthly existence.

Our mode of existence after death is largely unknown

Can these hints deprive death of its dreadful character? Not really. Death as the end of life is something very definite and vivid, whereas the hints of immortality point toward things totally unknown and totally unimaginable. We experience in a sharp and unmistakable way the sudden absence of the beloved person through death, the incomprehensible separation, the dreadful emptiness. A lifeless body that will quickly decay lies before us.

The soul (even though we know that it continues to exist) has been carried off into an impenetrable darkness. We cannot reach it; it cannot reach us. We know nothing of the *how* and *why* of its continued existence. Everything is puzzling, impenetrable, unimaginable.

In life our body and our soul, although each differs greatly from the other, partake of a unique *marriage*. It is precisely this intimate union which is ruptured in death as in no other way, not even in the prolonged loss of our consciousness.

So long as we go on living, our loss of consciousness in no way signifies the extinction of our soul. We might be in a state of shock caused by damage to our circulatory system; we might be under the influence of a powerful narcotic during surgery; we might even be in a month-long coma. But in all these cases, our soul still remains bound to our body. As soon as we regain consciousness, we are once again conscious human beings. Even if the return to normalcy is slow, as in the case of certain comas, we yet are headed toward the full consciousness of our identity, a matter of basic significance to us as persons.

The great riddle of death becomes grimly apparent when we compare the absence of the soul after death with the loss of consciousness of one still alive but barred from any conscious interaction with us. The unconscious soul may indeed be there but it is unreachable. Given that we ourselves have experienced such a loss of consciousness — a complete stilling of our consciousness, of that specific form of existence which constitutes us as a person — how shall we imagine the soul's continued existence? Just how does our soul exist when we undergo the complete loss of consciousness?

However this may be, as long as we continue to live in our body (which has this intimate link with our soul), our personal identity is continued. Our body is the bridge to our soul and, thus, to our personal identity. When we regain consciousness, we are able to take up again the inner awareness of our purely personal being. We are the same person as before, and we know it.

When at death the soul separates from the body, what happens to personal consciousness? Even on the natural plane, as I have argued, we can know that the soul continues to exist. This must mean, therefore, that when the soul definitively separates from the body, it does not descend into a night of unconsciousness. What a mystery is here! In life it is the body which plays a positive role in the continuity of our life as a person; it is this same body which at times can be the cause of our unconsciousness. And now, in death, when the body falls away from the soul, what becomes of the soul's consciousness?

IV

Death and the soul's relation to the body

THE Scholastics often discussed a man's love for his own body. St. Thomas Aquinas even has a curious interpretation of the command that a man should love his wife above all other humans. He argues that the Lord's statement "...and the two shall become one flesh"[21] is the basis for the husband's love of his wife; for, in loving her, he but loves his very own body.[22]

Our conscious and unconscious links to our body

In a previous work, I have shown that the solidarity each of us has with himself is not a fruit of love in any serious sense of the term.[23] It is rather something naturally given, something inevitable that does not belong to the moral sphere.

[21] Mt. 19:5.

[22] St. Thomas Aquinas, *Summa Theologica* 2a-2ae, q. 26, art. 11.

[23] Dietrich von Hildebrand, *Das Wesen der Liebe*, vol. III of *Gesammelte Werke* (Regensburg: Habbel, 1971), 19ff., 268 ff.

This is also true of our solidarity with our own body. It is not love that accounts for the fact that I feel a pain in my foot, that I experience something very unpleasant. There is simply an objective solidarity between myself and my bodily well-being.

But what is the situation concerning a consciously-assumed attitude toward my body? Does not this conscious posture go beyond the merely *objective* solidarity with self? My relation to my body is certainly unique. Gabriel Marcel goes so far as to deny that I *have* a body; he insists rather that I *am* my body.[24] But this surely is an exaggeration. I am not really my body in the same way that I am my soul — which is the very *I* that figures so radically in my life. Josef Seifert has grasped in a much deeper and more accurate way than Marcel the precise link between the self, the soul, and the body.[25]

In any case, our purpose here is to focus on my conscious attachment to my body which goes beyond the matter-of-fact *objective* solidarity which I have with my own body, but which is still not love in any true sense of the term. I place, for example, a high value on my hand, my leg, or my whole body. This becomes especially noticeable if I should lose a hand or should be forced to have my leg amputated. Even such a great ascetic as St. Francis of Assisi, who used to castigate "Brother Ass" (the name by which he referred to his body) was attached to his body in a conscious way.

This attachment to our own body, the high point of *what is mine*, assumes a special form when it concerns our senses, especially sight and hearing. How significant is our ability to

---

[24] *"Je suis mon corps."* Gabriel Marcel, *Le Mystère de l'Être* (Paris: Aubier, 1951), vol. 1, lesson 5, 116, 119-20.

[25] Josef Seifert, *Leib und Seele* (Salzburg: Anton Pustet, 1973), 336 ff., n. 453.

see! How much are we indebted to our eyes for their unique contact with the world around us, above all with other persons and with the inexhaustible world of visible beauty! And what joy is ours from our sense of hearing! What gifts of God are our senses, nay, our entire body!

My body is an objective good for me

Meditating on the above makes one fact clear: our body, as a whole and in its individual parts, is an objective blessing for us. In our attachment to our body, therefore, our response to this blessing and its value is most important. Going beyond the merely objective solidarity with self, our response is a very real, meaningful attitude that has a certain analogy with love.

In my relationship to another person, that person's body also plays a great role, one that is quite different from the relationship that I have with my own body. The other's body belongs to her in such a way that it determines in many ways my contact with her. How important is her bodily presence! How wonderful that I hear her voice, that I see the form and face which express her very soul!

Above all, if I love someone in a special way, then I love also her body, especially her face. The great esteem I feel for her personality makes me value also her body. In the love that forms the heart of marriage, the body of my spouse acquires an added meaning: I love her body in the fullest sense, with a genuine love. For, shining forth from her body is the mystery that "in this vessel abides the one I love most of all."[26]

[26] This context (of death and the dreadful separation of soul from body) does not permit further exploration into the meaning of the various parts of the body. I must forego, therefore, a fuller analysis of the eyes

My body can be be experienced as a prison for my soul

My death involves the complete separation of my soul from my body. This is reason enough to dread death, to regard it as a great misfortune. Nevertheless, we need to balance this truth with an insight that Plato so wonderfully emphasized, namely, that the body is also a *prison for the soul*. A great and mysterious inequality is found in the linkage between my soul and my body. My soul belongs to an incomparably superior ontological sphere than does my body. My entire personal and conscious being is rooted in my soul. It is my soul which underlies the total fullness of my sensory acts; it is my soul which knows, understands, loves, and exercises free will.

And yet — strange truth! — my life as a person depends on my body to the extent that the normal functioning of my brain is an essential requirement of personal consciousness even though it is not the *cause* of it. To a considerable extent I am dependent on my body. Bodily pains and discomforts can burden me to such a degree that I can experience my body, not as an objective blessing, but as a misfortune. Indeed, weariness and exhaustion can hinder the full development of my personal life. For such reasons it thus becomes comprehensible to speak of my body as a *prison for my soul*.

In this naive *existential* aspect of death which we have just considered, we grasp that death cuts us off from everything we know, from the entire world around us. After death we are no

of a person, the mouth, or the unclothed body and the whole realm of intimacy. My task here is to distinguish our attitude toward our own body from our attitude toward that of another. I have also sought to show how death means one thing when it concerns the separation of my soul from my body, and another thing when it concerns the soul and body of another, especially a beloved person.

longer in the same universe. Our natural ignorance about the fate of the soul after death goes so far that we have no idea what knowledge about this world survives in the soul of someone who has died.

V

Man's metaphysical grandeur
— and death's second natural aspect

WE come now to a second natural aspect of death, which I shall call the *metaphysical aspect*. To see it clearly, we must briefly consider man's unique powers in contrast to all other earthly creatures, and then, if only briefly, let shine forth the whole fullness of the world which we know and in which we live.

Against this background, death will reveal a different aspect. Death's cutting us off from our metaphysical grandeur will constitute a new woe, to be added to the pitiful state of our body when the soul departs.

The metaphysical aspect of death

We humans on this earthly pilgrimage — in *statu viae* — have been granted a magnificent boon: essentially related to our personal existence is the power of having a *perspective* on the universe. Of all earthly creatures, we alone can grasp other things and know what we have perceived. We can understand them. We alone can think and speak. We alone can have real community with others. We are able to perceive others as spiritual beings, to speak to them, and to understand their replies. We can make requests of others, turn to them in a significant way, question them. With others we can accomplish a mutual glance of love or achieve a deep and blissful union. In a splendid passage in *Antigone*, Sophocles says of humanity: "Wonders are many, but none is more wonderful than man!"[27]

By far the highest human privilege and gift is our ability to accept God, to be *capax Dei*. To this end we humans have free will and are able to bear moral values such as justice and piety, generosity and truthfulness.

The metaphysical vs. the naive natural aspect of death

We are now in a position to contrast the metaphysical aspect of death with the naive natural aspect. This latter focuses on the universe as something quantitatively incomparably greater than any man. It is from this that man is separated by death. How tiny and insignificant is any man in contrast to the universe! How much we humans do not know, do not understand! A single human spirit seems dwarfed by the incredibly rich and varied universe before him. And when a man dies, this entire universe goes down before his very eyes! Thus Pascal emphasizes the fragility of a man: a drop of water can kill him.[28]

---

[27] Sophocles, *Antigone*, act 1, line 332.

[28] "Man is but a reed, the most feeble thing in nature; but he is a thinking reed. The entire universe need not arm itself to crush him. A vapor, a drop of water suffices to kill him. But, if the universe were to crush him, man would still be more noble than that which killed him, because he knows that he dies and the advantage which the universe has over him; the universe knows nothing of this." Blaise Pascal, *Pensées*, trans. W.F.

But Pascal emphasizes still more the other side of this mystery, the metaphysical side. The universe, for all its dizzying might and awesome, frightening powers, does not know that it is snuffing out a personal existence. But the person, the otherwise pitiful victim, does know. And therein lies his superiority to the whole material universe. Pascal with his few words has captured the ambivalence of our human condition: on the one hand, the fragility and seeming inconsequence of a human life; on the other, the great superiority of personal existence.

Something analogous to Pascal's point is our own, namely, the fearsome rupture which death brings about between our personal consciousness and the broad range of the world around us. While we live, we enjoy many different contacts with the world. We perceive many parts of it, know and understand different beings in it. Above all, we enter into manifold and deep relations with other persons.

All this is ruptured by death. Death, as it were, slays the entire universe.

In the world around us we encounter a contrast of still another kind. On the one hand, so many things lift up our heart and stir within us great happiness. They contain a message — the promise of eternity. On the other hand, however, other things in the universe depress us, overwhelm us in a somewhat fearful way. Pascal is thinking of just these things when he writes of his terror before the immensity of the universe and all the countless galaxies.[29]

There are, to be sure, still other contrasts, other ambiguities. An especially poignant one is the contrast between the fleeting

Trotter, vol. 33 of *The Great Books of the Western World* (Chicago: Encyclopedia Britannica, 1952), VI, 347.

[29] *Pensées*, II, 72.

existence — the transiency — of earthly things, and the hints of eternity which somehow filter through to us. Transiency has to do with the birth and death of living things, with the rhythm of time, above all with human instability. Against the permanence of eternity, transiency reveals how even the most beautiful and blissful moments of life are hurled inevitably into the past.

The superiority of the person over the universe

But the contrast we must deal with here is not that between the transient things of time and the permanence of eternity; it is rather that between the tiny, helpless reality of a spiritual person and the immensity of space with its unnumbered stars and its well-nigh infinite dimensions. Taken quantitatively, the frightening size and silence of the material universe oppress us; they offer a brutal contrast to our smallness and apparent insignificance.

Although the mere dimensions of matter in space are in fact relatively superficial when compared to the depth and worth of a spiritual person, yet they present themselves as gigantically superior. As Pascal says in his *Pensées*, "The eternal silence of these infinite spaces terrifies me."[30]

When we focus just on the worth and mystery of the person — this unique spiritual being that inhabits the earth — we are far removed from the oppressiveness of the immensity of the material universe. The person is open to all the great blessings of life: the moral values of other persons, the great beauty in nature and in art, the stirring metaphysical truths which form

[30] *Pensées*, III, 206.

the background of our pilgrimage through time, the blissful experience of loving another and being loved in return. These blessings are not just directed to us as individuals in a private way. On the contrary, they prove by their very existence the superiority of the spiritual and personal over the quantitative immensity of the material universe. What is more, they contain a direct promise which lifts up our soul in hope. They point to an eternity which will be for us the fulfillment of what on earth speaks so significantly and happily now.

These great earthly experiences somehow guarantee that the personal and the spiritual will triumph over the material; that what is in fact both ontologically and existentially superior in value will not be defeated by the merely quantitatively superior.

The two natural aspects of death compared

Our natural understanding of death, therefore, holds out before us two very different aspects: on the one hand, our fearful going down into nothingness; on the other, our transition to a higher form of personal existence based on the natural certainty of immortality — on the "promises" from beyond.

The first aspect emphasizes the misfortune of death insofar as it severs our many ties to the inexhaustible realities of earthly life. We do not know how this severance occurs; we know only that death is a radical break with the whole real world around us.

The other aspect emphasizes the promise of a better life beyond the grave. It reads the many messages of hope conveyed by earthly blessings such as love, truth, and beauty. In a hushed voice, as it were, it whispers to us that our souls will not die. But even under this bright aspect we face the darkness of the unknown. Where are we transported to? What is the form of our new existence there? After we die, what relationship exists between our former earthly life and our existence in eternity?

On the natural level the answers to these questions are unknown, are completely impenetrable and unimaginable. The promises of great future blessings point only to the great value of the soul's existence and to the continuance of this existence. About everything else, there is silence and great mystery.

VI

The longing for death

WE have so far considered death from the natural point of view and have spoken of it as an inevitable misfortune threatening all of us: we fear it as a great evil. But do not many people yearn for death? Have there not always been suicides? And are not suicides increasing to a frightful degree today?

We must now consider the undeniable fact that death, which seems to be so universally feared, is nevertheless welcomed by so many. We will have to turn, therefore, to the different reasons why people long for death and why so many of them take their own lives.

Our lives are in God's hands

First, however, we must stress above all the fact that we humans are in God's hands, that He alone must decide when we shall die. In death we are touched by God in a unique way. Unlike so many events in our earthly life, death neither includes nor depends on our free cooperation: we *undergo* death.

Jaws of Death: Gate of Heaven

God alone is the Lord of life and death. Essentially linked to this truth is another one: on the purely natural plane, death can dominate us. Once it has occurred, there is no way to reverse it.

But is it not within our power to deprive another human of life? Can we not intervene and cause the death of another? Certainly. But this possibility — and frightening actuality — has no significance when we realize that God alone has the right to dispose of innocent human life.

Legitimate human authority, of course, acting as God's partial representative on earth, may punish certain crimes with death. And we may lawfully kill an aggressor in self-defense. But a frightful wrong, a very serious sin occurs when we take the life of an innocent person of our own free will.

The same sin is present when we take our own life. Murder and suicide thus are indeed possible and available to us — yet only in the same way as are other sins. Their being *possible* does not change the fact that to God alone belongs the right to rule human life and death. Murder and suicide directly attack the high value of human life and are sins for this very reason. Murder is the most extreme form of irreverence and lack of love. As Plato argued,[31] when we commit murder, we usurp a right that belongs to God alone.

In the case of a death sentence imposed by the state, we have quite a different situation because the state acts as a genuine authority, that is, as a partial proxy for God. Also, in the case of our killing someone who attacks us, we have an action based on the right to self-defense that is expressly granted to human beings.

---

[31] *Phaedo*, 61E ff.

The longing for death

Very different motives can account for the longing for death that some persons experience. Each confers its own specific character on death. A man's basic view of death, moreover, will vary decisively according to the specific kind of motive that engages him.

Suffering, hopelessness, and dread as motives

There is, first of all, the yearning for death brought on by various kinds of suffering. Life for many persons means an unending succession of fearful mental and physical sufferings. If we think of the continual bodily and mental tortures so vividly detailed by Solzhenitsyn in his accounts of the Soviet Gulag, we can well appreciate how death must appear as something desirable to the hapless prisoners. Death will be seen as the end of suffering and as a kind of redemption from an intolerable life.[32] So too, death will be found attractive by those enduring unbearable pain as the result of an incurable illness.

A second motive for the yearning for death is hopelessness. A man may find himself in a painfully humiliating situation from which he cannot disentangle himself. He may believe that his own efforts will avail him nothing, that the situation is hopeless.

A third motive is dread. Intense fear in the face of grave dangers can trigger panic, which in turn may create a longing for death.

---

[32] Alexander Solzhenitsyn, *The Gulag Archipelago, 1918-1956: An Experiment in Literary Investigation* (New York: Harper & Row, 1978).

Liberation is a common theme in the longing for death

The longing for death takes on a different character with each of the different motives operating. The first case, involving frightful bodily or mental tortures, presents us with a motive which comes much closer to a strict longing for death than do the other two cases. Common to all the cases, however, is the fact that death is sought after primarily as a liberation. Thus death is narrowly understood, grasped only in its relation to the cessation of certain earthly torments or as an escape from a hopeless situation.

The longing for death here, therefore, does not necessarily include any kind of position as to what happens after death. Death is desired, nay, is yearned for, no matter whether the concerned person sees it as a going down into nothingness[33] or as a higher form of the continued existence of the soul. Liberation is the dominant aspect.[34]

---

[33] People with a single-minded focus on this aspect of liberation (who regard death only as a redemption from unbearable sufferings and at the same time consider death to be a going down into nothingness), are obviously blind to the dreadfulness of nonexistence. As a result, the true aspect of death is totally concealed from them. They do not understand that the loss of our personal existence is the greatest misfortune, as St. Augustine states so magnificently.

[34] In ancient times suicide was not always regarded as something prohibited for moral reasons. Quite the contrary! The suicides of Lucretia and of Cato were thought to be acts of admirable courage. Only in the monotheistic world of the Old and New Testaments is suicide always seen as something morally prohibited, indeed, as something evil. Schopenhauer defends suicide to the point of claiming that it is thoroughly unobjectionable. Cf. Arthur Schopenhauer, *The World as Will and Idea* (I, 69) and his *Parerga and Paralipomena*, II, 13 ("On Suicide").

Spiritual despair can be a motive for suicide

Quite different is the case where the longing for death is motivated by spiritual despair about the world or about life as a whole. Thus the young Jacques Maritain and his wife, Raissa, were in such despair over the philosophical teachings of the positivists at the Sorbonne concerning the relativity of all truth, that they decided to take their own lives. A life without the possibility of absolute truth seemed to them not worth living.[35]

They had already agreed on the day and the hour of their mutual suicides when they met with the teaching and personality of the eminent philosopher, Henri Bergson. He convinced them that objective truth exists. He gave them hope of discovering it. For the Maritains before they met Bergson, therefore, as well as for all those who seek death for similar reasons, death means the cessation — not of intolerable sufferings in this life — but of life itself. It probably means a simple going down into nothingness.

Despair over the total aspect of this valley of tears was obviously also the basic motive for the suicide of the noted German writer Heinrich von Kleist (1777-1811). Kant's philosophy with its *transcendental subjectivism* played a great role in his deep dejection and despair. We do not know whether death for Kleist meant a simple going down into nothingness, but in any case it seemed to him primarily the longed-for abandonment of a life no longer worth living.

---

[35] Raissa Maritain, *We Have Been Friends Together* (New York: Longmans, Green, 1943), chap. 3.

Suicide as a means to reunion with a deceased loved one

The longing for death has still a different character when it is a response to the death of someone we love very deeply. Death itself takes on a different hue in each of its several aspects. In this instance, we may long for death because the worst and most frightful natural misfortune has befallen us. From the natural point of view, we are afflicted with the greatest and deepest loss possible to humans.

This particular yearning for death has an especially noble character, born of love and of love's tears and grief. It stands in sharp contrast to the yearning motivated by the radical error of the relativity of all truth.

To suffer and to yearn for death because "truth does not exist" — as understandable as this may be, especially in our times of intellectual giddiness and nonsense — is at bottom an unfounded response, an answer to an objectively baseless concern, precisely because truth *does* exist.

But our suffering over the death of a loved one is something totally different. It is, in fact, an adequate answer. Our beloved is dead. Our bereavement, from the natural point of view, does really call for an anguished yearning for radical relief.

When bereavement is the motive, our yearning for death is also implicitly bound up with our certainty about the continued existence of the soul in the life beyond. This yearning, in fact, presupposes the belief that there shall be a reunion with our beloved in eternity.

Yet our yearning for death in such cases does not lead to thoughts of suicide. In fact, our faith in God and our hope for a blessed reunion with our loved one in eternity cannot be separated from our consciousness of the dreadful sin of suicide. That we hope to be reunited with our beloved in eternity demands, indeed, our prior belief in God and in the eternal bliss rooted in our attaining Him. Such a hope understands the unique sin of suicide to be an obstacle to our finding our beloved again.

Even so, suicides do occur because of the death of a loved one. A certain despair of mind plays a great role here. Suicide can be planned — and accomplished — even by one who is a true believer and who understands that suicide is a serious sin. (I knew a young man who wore a scapular of the Carmelite religious order. In a note written before taking his own life, he asked God for forgiveness.)

Thus, we may agree that most suicides spring from deep mental disturbances but we must also bear in mind that suicides can spring from the coexistence in the mind of contradictory ideas.

There is a great difference between *essential laws* underlying all personal existence and the *psychological possibilities* which are mysteriously available to humans whereby all sorts of conflicting and irrational ideas can crowd together within the same mind and drive it to what are objectively absurd and contradictory decisions.[36]

In the face of all that he believes and hopes for, the bereaved man may surrender to the urge to take his own life.[37] As always,

---

[36] A fuller discussion of this mysterious fact is beyond the scope of this present book. It must suffice that we note its existence as a tentative, if incomplete, explanation for some suicides. Cf. Dietrich von Hildebrand, *Moralia*, vol. 9 of *Gesammelte Werke* (Regensburg: Habbel, 1980), chap. 22.

[37] It is noteworthy that even those who do not regard death as an evil to be feared but rather as something that frees them from great suffering (especially suffering over the loss of a loved one) still have an instinct for self-preservation. If they are in mortal danger or if death threatens to destroy them, they may often seek in an instinctive way to save their own lives.

suicide here is a dreadful evil even when death is not sought for its own sake, but as a gateway leading to reunion with a loved one![38]

[38] I do not wish to elaborate upon all the different aspects of death with respect to their unique characteristics. Even so, I must mention briefly a view of death as friendly liberator which can be misleading. For example, Schubert's moving song *Der Tod und das Mädchen* ("Death and the Young Girl") does not present death as something gruesome or frightful, to be avoided under all circumstances. It is not portrayed as a calamity toward which we all draw near, reluctantly and inevitably. Rather, this song depicts death as a bestower of gentle rest, a liberation from all earthly suffering, and from all fear and uncertainty.

As a poetic approach, the aspect presented by the song has a certain merit since it does have a basis in fact. But the approach is flawed and obviously one-sided. Above all, it is incompatible with the Christian and supernatural view of death. In no way does it take into account the fact that death is a punishment. It is not at all that view of death found at the heart of St. Paul's stirring, triumphant charge: "O death, where is thy sting?"(1 Cor. 15:15).

Again, at the end of his splendid *Canticle of the Sun*, St. Francis of Assisi sings about "Brother Death." Here he points to a quite unique aspect of death. This beautiful aspect, which can certainly be harmonized with the supernatural and Christian view of death, nonetheless contains a certain note which can easily be misunderstood if it is separated from St. Francis' total view of all creation. As it stands, the view in the *Canticle* is not *necessarily* related to the Christian view, nor does it belong necessarily to that classical formulation (in Matthew 25:6) which should surpass and redeem the natural view of death for Christians: "Behold, the Bridegroom cometh!"

Therefore, the view of death in the *Canticle* is not directly related to our subject. Cf. Dietrich von Hildebrand, *Der Geist des hl. Franziskus und der dritte Orden* (Munich: Theatiner-Verlag, 1921): "Der Geist des hl. Franziskus," II, 13 ff.; and "Der heilige Franziskus von Assisi" in *Die Menschheit am Scheideweg* (Regensburg: Habbel, 1955), 504, 506.

VII

Our solitude in death

DEATH is extraordinarily intimate. Despite the fact that all men must undergo this common, mysterious fate at one time or another, death is still in a special way a most individual matter for each of us. Death comes to everyone as a totally intimate and personal fate. It is a basic element of each human's destiny.

However different our lives may be in all other respects, each of us shares the fate of death with all our fellow humans. At the same time, death is most intimate. It concerns each of us in a totally unique and individual way. Each human being must be prepared for his own death; each feels anxiety precisely over the inevitable occurrence of his own death.

When he learned from the prophet Isaiah that the hour of his death had come, King Hezekiah turned in his bed toward the wall and wept bitterly.[39] This passage from the Old Testament clearly shows us two things: death is a dreadful misfortune

---

[39] 4 Kings 20:1 ff.

for humanity, and death is simultaneously a most intimate affair for each of us individually.

The solitary grandeur of death

Death offers a striking contrast to all that is ungenuine and unnecessary. It has a solitary and authentic grandeur. Much that is worthless may exist somehow tied up with each of us, although by no means in the same degree. But death, with its uniqueness and singularity, with its deep significance and ultimate reality, forms a deep contrast to all the vanities and empty and false attitudes which surround our separate existences. I refer to the errors which grip us, but also to the dangers we merely imagine, to the "wounds" we may think we have received from the insensitivity of others; I refer also to the many transient and insignificant actions which fill so many hours in our lives.

When a man dies, quite apart from his condition at the time, there shines forth in a special way his nobility as a human being. His death, and the death of each of us, has something about it that is grand, genuine, and significant. In death, a man partakes of something mysterious and great, something ultimately serious and noble, despite all the dread we have of it. This noble aspect of death implies the continuance in existence of the human soul and, indirectly, even the supernatural view of death. It surfaces less by the thought of our own death than by the death of someone else, especially if the latter has a great significance in our life.

Certain musical settings, such as the Verdi *Requiem* or the plainsong in a Gregorian *Requiem Mass*, clearly express death's majesty and manifest its ceremonial authenticity. What is expressed is the very opposite of the queen's banal view in

Shakespeare's *Hamlet*: "Thou know'st 'tis common; all that lives must die."[40]

Our absolute isolation in death

Besides these "positive" aspects of death, there is also an isolation that is fearful and extremely negative: each of us must die his own death. Death, moreover, places us in absolute isolation with respect to every form of human companionship. In our act of dying we cannot include the one we love most deeply. To be sure, we can die in her arms and allow our love to flow out toward her with our last breath. But still we die alone.

This *death in isolation* is, of course, death as seen from the human, the natural perspective. From the supernatural perspective, death can be seen as the beginning of a quite new form of association with God. As we shall see in some detail later, in the expression "Behold, the Bridegroom cometh!,"[41] there lies the fulfillment of our basic relation to the One for whom we have been created: the commencement of our association in love with God, face to face. For now, however, we continue to speak about the purely natural aspect of death, which entails an absolute isolation — a dreadful solitude — as its tragic component.

The joint death of two lovers as a fulfillment of love

We sometimes encounter in philosophy and theology a datum which involves a mysterious *coincidentia oppositorum* — *a meeting of opposites*. We must now apply this to death itself.

[40] *Hamlet*, act 1, sc. 2, lines 72-73.
[41] Mt. 25:6.

Despite the fact that death unfolds in an ultimate solitude, still the joint death of two lovers involves a unique form of fulfill-ment for their relationship.

This point shall become clear after we take up once again the positive aspect of death, namely, its great solemnity. A special significance attaches to death as our ultimate, valid *statement* — in contrast to all the other acts we have carried out in life. Its ultimacy and absolute uniqueness cannot be com-pared to any other part of our life.[42]

Such a view is realized in the classical desire of lovers to die together. They desire not only to escape being separated by death, but also to perform together the personal act of dying which, in and of itself, is solitary, definitive, and important. In a word, they desire to make the ultimate and valid *affirmation* together. In countless classical songs, and even in popular bal-lads, we encounter this desire for dying together on the part of two lovers. This desire highlights a most interesting and novel aspect of death.

All love involves an ardent *intentio unionis*, a desire to be united with the loved one in whatever ways the particular love in question entails. In the desire for a joint death, the *intentio unionis* uniquely and conclusively aims at carrying out together this most important moment, this final and decisive act. A shared death here thus seems to be something positive, a mys-terious fulfillment of one of love's great *intentions*. Out of a deeply solitary act, such a shared death achieves a special fulfillment of the highest and most intimate relationship.

---

[42] As we shall see in detail later on, this view of death takes on still another fresh significance from the standpoint of the supernatural and Christian framework.

The special bliss of a shared death is most beautifully expressed in the last scene of Verdi's opera *Aida*. Radames, condemned to death because of his activity on behalf of Aida's father, suddenly discovers that Aida has let herself be walled up in a tomb with him. His fear of death and his frightful suffering at being separated from her are then transfigured by their shared death.

We find something quite novel in Wagner's masterpiece *Tristan and Isolde*. The theme of this opera is the mutual love of two human beings who, in the end, take love and the *intentio unionis* of love so seriously that they find the earthly situation of humanity to be incompatible with the total fulfillment of their love.

Genuine mystics know of a similar contrast between earthly, everyday activity and the eternal, unbroken, and ultimate love communion with Jesus. But Wagner's opera is not concerned with such ultimates; nor does it deal with mankind's true reason for existence — its *raison d'être* — which can only be the union in love of each of us with the God-Man, that union which alone can bring us eternal happiness. Wagner's opera, instead, is more concerned with the earthly situation which is hostile to Tristan's ecstatic union with the woman he loves. Instead of being allowed to remain in the blissful eternal present, the lovers are forced always to return to the periphery, to develop according to the rhythm of time.

I am far from saying that the lovers in this opera are correct in every respect. They are in fact radically at odds with the deepest implications of our earthly situation, for their human relationship is such that it excludes their eternal union with Jesus. An abyss separates their world of merely human love from man's final union of love with Jesus; but their world nevertheless has deeply similar moments with the latter.

For the ecstasy of love has a fervor, an intensity, and a depth that are incomparably superior to everything else. Tristan and Isolde, consequently, are correct when they feel that their love, strained to the very utmost and directed toward their full ecstatic union, cannot attain complete fulfillment in this earthly life. They rightly feel the antagonism of the workaday world to their love. They rightly yearn for the situation of eternity, in which they will be able to live only for love.

The two lovers' feelings are correct to the extent that they grasp the incompatibility of love with our earthly situation. But their feelings are obviously incorrect to the extent that they fail to understand that our ultimate theme as human beings is not union with another human person (however strong our love may be), but union with Jesus and, in Him and through Him, union with God the Father.

It is most important for us to focus on this view of death which sees death as a means to escape the limitations placed on love by earthly existence and as a means to achieve a blessed elevation into the undisturbed fulfillment of an ecstatic love. In this view, death is not a frightful process of growing numb, not a going down into nothingness. Nor is it a puzzling, painful farewell to all our loved ones. Nor again is it absolute solitude. Death rather becomes a fulfillment, which clearly presupposes the continued existence of the soul.

The view of death in *Tristan and Isolde* is thus in radical opposition to the view which I have called the *naive natural view*, whereby death presents the frightful character of a going down into nothingness. It is in opposition also to the view that longs for death only as a liberation from our intolerable sufferings and does not conceive death as a fulfillment and a form of bliss. But, notwithstanding the completely *positive* view of death given in Wagner's opera, there still remains the great mystery of what happens after death and the great question of whether the soul indeed continues to live after the body dies.

We should also note that the aspect of death in *Tristan and Isolde* differs greatly from the Socratic conviction that the continuation of the soul's existence is certain, and that its separation from the body is a genuine liberation. Socrates looked upon death as the beginning of a higher spiritual existence in which we achieve a higher and purer *gazing at Ideas;* we might almost speak of a *gazing at God.*

Because of the emphasis placed on love, the aspect of death which Wagner puts forward in *Tristan and Isolde* has something resembling the view of the genuine mystic. Like the mystic's view, it understands eternity as a form of ecstasy.[43]

But from another standpoint, the view of Socrates comes closer to the Christian mystic's view, for the goal of both Socrates and the Christian mystic is God alone, the pure contemplation of the Divine Absolute.

---

[43] Appendix A gives further consideration to the view of death found in *Tristan and Isolde*.

VIII

The unnatural character of death

WHEN, however, we turn away from the exceptional case of the joint death of two lovers and return to the natural aspect of death, we encounter again man's dread of death, man's awareness that it is the fate of humans to dwell in the shadow of death. This dread becomes much clearer when we emphasize death's contrast to the bounty of earthly life.

Life's bounty and the puzzling darkness of death

I am thinking here, of course, of the great blessings of life, when immense gifts are showered down upon us; but I am also thinking of the human soul, so full of hope for real happiness. There is a charm to life, a kind of magic. Blessings actually received or ardently desired make our lives attractive, pleasant, and intoxicating.

Many of us have experienced in our own youth something of the magic sweetness which Hans Sachs expresses in Wagner's *Die Meistersinger*:

Jaws of Death: Gate of Heaven

Mein Freund! in holder Jugendzeit,
Wenn uns von mächt'gen Trieben
Zum sel'gen ersten Lieben
Die Brust sich schwellet hoch und weit,
Ein schönes Lied zu singen
Mocht' vielen da gelingen.[44]

O friend, in the springtime of youth,
When our breast swells high with desire,
When love first sets the heart on fire,
The urge in many is so strong
To raise their voice in song.

To be sure, we are not all so blessed as to have experienced fully this wondrous aspect of life. Many of us are too dull to feel the magic, to be fully awake to the promise of happiness and to the mysterious longings of the youthful soul. On the other hand, some others — especially those who are *chosen* — are intent upon God and the things of God from the very beginning. Jesus has touched their hearts in such a way that the charm of life, by contrast, pales into insignificance; their desire for earthly happiness is quite surpassed by their ardent longing to follow Jesus and become transformed in Him.

There exists also another class of persons whose souls retain to some degree a certain normal, happy view of life but whose fate crushes any possibility of fulfillment. A special suffering has been placed between them and a happy earthly life. Perhaps a serious bodily illness prevents them from any kind of enjoyment; or, as prisoners in a concentration camp, they have been

---

[44] *Die Meistersinger*, act 3, sc. 2.

cut off from all of life's blessings. They may, of course, continue to think longingly of the magic promises of life, but the actual daily routine of life has been changed for them into a Hell.

Throughout this discussion of the bounty of life, I am thinking of the inexhaustible charm offered by the fullness of life's blessings, its surprises, its happy and mysterious rhythms. I absolutely exclude all phony charms and any false magic of life — all the attempts to desecrate life's blessings so as to misuse and misunderstand them, all the perversions of good things which destroy the possibility of their bringing us real happiness. I also exclude the deceptive charm which life possesses for reckless, superficial individuals, above all of the Don Giovanni type.

No, I am thinking of the bountiful charm and intoxication, the magical awareness which finds artistic expression in Shakespeare's *As You Like It*. It is the magic which inspires Goethe's poem, *"Wie herrlich leuchtet mir die Natur!"*[45] It is the same wondrous, intoxicating charm which is found in so many episodes of Cervantes' *Don Quixote*.

Such a view of life places us in a warm and loving contact with the ambience of a situation, with the different *worlds* it may offer us. We are alive to all of life's joys and its sense of celebration, to all the things permeated by a truly comic spirit. We are able to touch life's mysteries, ranging from the changes of the seasons and the day's changes (from morning through noon into evening) to the mysterious and sublime forms of human relations.

To grasp all these wonders demands a special sensory ability as well as a special alertness. Life indeed presents all these

[45] "How Splendidly Nature Glows to Me!" Goethe, *Mailied.*

wondrous aspects. Its charm, sweetness, and beauty are objectively rooted in the reality of life. Despite the undeniable reality
of sorrows in this valley of tears, we are entitled to cry out, "How
lovely you are, O world! How sweet is life!"

The darkness of death overshadows life's bounty

This legitimate aspect, despite many disappointments and
frustrations, has, as I have insisted, its own basis in reality. But
now let us think of death. In death all of these lovely things
suddenly fade away. The radiant appearances of the earth and
all its sweet expectations cease. New aspects of life appear,
uncanny and disturbing. The darkness of death replaces the
brightness and sweetness of life. We become aware of a solemn,
heartbreaking contrast.

Death's shadow varies according to the threats we face

The awareness of this contrast differs according to the nature
of the threats to our life. Thus, an innocent person condemned
to death experiences the threat of death differently than does
someone whose life is endangered by fire, shipwreck, or serious
illness.

The difference I mean to stress here is the following: there
are cases where a man in the full flower of life is threatened by
a great external danger. On the other hand, there are cases
when our lives fade away, when a serious illness draws us ever
closer to an imminent death. In the first cases we experience
the contrast between a full life and the sudden cessation of
everything around us, of everything we are in body and in soul.
In the second cases, we experience but a constant decline. We
die more and more each day.

The unnatural character of death

Our general awareness that death is inevitable

Another distinction must be stressed, i.e, that between a *particular* awareness of death because of some imminent, threatening cause and a *general* awareness throughout our lifetime that death is inevitable, that it draws nearer to us with each breath we take.

In the latter case, our concern is not with the contrast between the fullness of life and the threat of its sudden and perhaps unexpected termination, nor with the contrast between life's fullness and the ever-declining strength of body which afflicts us when we are gripped by a mortal illness. Rather, we are simply focused on the clear fact that *someday we must die*. Death cannot be escaped; it is the earthly future for each one of us. The certainty of our death is matched by our equal uncertainty as to when and where death will snatch away our earthly existence: *"Media in vita mortis sumus."* ("We live out our lives in the very midst of death.")[46]

It is this general awareness of death which I have in mind when I speak of death's natural aspect. Its tragic, sad message belongs to our metaphysical situation as human beings. The general awareness of death is an essential part of the puzzling contrast that characterizes our earthly life.

On the one hand, the world around us is so full of immense blessings that we are moved to join our voices to the angels' hymn, "Heaven and earth are filled with Thy glory!"[47]

On the other hand, there is the inescapable fact that we live in a valley of tears. Tragedy exists in the midst of the fundamental splendor of the world. The dark hues of tragedy mock and

[46] From a Latin antiphon composed by Notker of St. Gall.
[47] *Gloria* of the Mass: *"Pleni sunt coeli et terra gloria tua!"*

threaten the radiant blessings of life — the beauty, truth, and goodness which surround us. Tragedy sets itself against God's countless wonders, above all against our heritage of Paradise and human love in all its natural forms.

Our mortal condition — our being inevitably subject to the doom of death — is essentially bound to the rhythm of time, which relentlessly hurls the present into the past. We understand the impossibility of clinging to a happy *today*.

Worse still, our mortal condition is joined by the many depressing evils which coexist with death: the horrible sins committed each day, the triumph of devilish errors, the ominous spread of false teachings, the countless sufferings and sorrows of the innocent. These add their frightful, ugly hues to those of death; they make still more mysterious and depressing the contrast with life's radiant glow and wondrous beauty.

Death is not a natural transition, but a radical break

Death is not some normal termination for humanity, like a matter-of-fact progression from childhood to adulthood, from youth to manhood. Man's life-process is indeed achieved over time. There are the stages of life, from child to adult to old man. There is an ascent unto the full vigor of manhood and then a decline. But in the aspect of death afforded to us by merely natural experience, death remains an abrupt event, puzzling and incomprehensible. When we make the fearful transition from earthly life to death, we are cut off from association with other humans, from all kinds of blessings, from all kinds of knowledge, and from the real world around us.

Death means the radical disappearance of all these things; it brings us to a condition of absolute isolation. Such a radical break is just as puzzling — and as fearful — as the contrast between earthly life with its splendor and earthly life as a valley of tears.

I have already quoted the contrast noted by Pascal: "Man is but a reed, the most feeble thing in nature, but he is a thinking reed."[48] This contrast deals with the fact that bearers of high values are far more fragile than lower beings. This same contrast — between value and power — is clearly reflected in Plato's *Phaedrus* by his metaphor of the white steed and the black one.[49] There is, thus, an evident lack of harmony in the cosmos. There is a puzzling and depressing lack of proportion between a being's preciousness and its fragility. It seems as if brute irrational forces have been allowed to trample upon the wondrous but too-vulnerable higher beings. Holy Scripture reveals this disharmony to be the result of Original Sin. In a certain way, in death we find concentrated the fearful contrast that permeates the whole cosmos and human life. In death, life's intoxicating beauty, God's countless gifts, and the many sources of happiness all come up against our valley of tears.

Death separates us from all that we love

From the earthly point of view, death means farewell to all the most precious natural blessings, most especially farewell to all the persons we love. Death lights up everything beneficial and beautiful which we must abandon forever. Gazing upon these good things to which we must bid a relentless farewell, we are touched with a mysterious, heart-rending pain. So many things parade before us in their strange contrasts, their competing claims: our need to depart at some time from the earth but

[48] *Pensées*, VI, 347.
[49] *Phaedrus*, 253D ff.

also our inner claim on a continued existence; the fact of death surrounding everything earthly but so, too, the promise of eternity (which everything great and beautiful suggests to us, hinting of God).

The sorrow of separation from those whom we love

Dreadful on two accounts is the farewell we must take from those persons we love deeply, most especially from the one person we love beyond everyone else. First, our own heart breaks to be torn from the one who is the source of our joy and happiness. Death carries us away into an unknown dark land, where we can no longer find our beloved, where she has disappeared from our sight. Death ends our blessed relationship.

Second, death is dreadful because of the anguish we cause our beloved. Our most ardent wish was to bestow happiness upon her, and now our death ruptures our love communion. In a certain way, our own death is the greatest misfortune for our beloved. I say "in a certain way," because from another point of view, our beloved would suffer an even greater misfortune if we ceased to love her and turned our heart away from her.

The misfortune of our death, of course, is not our fault. We are forced against our will to abandon her. Even so, we are only too conscious that our death will be something dreadful for her. Our fault or not, our death will bring her grief.

In death, we leave behind both time and space

The world around us is immensely real and it is inseparably linked to space. The earthly life of each one of us is just as inseparably linked to time. In death the soul of a human person leaves this world of space and time. Only the body remains, still somehow positioned in the world of space. It will be burned or it will in time disintegrate in the grave. The place to which our soul goes cannot be reached by thought. Where is Heaven? Where is Purgatory? Where is Hell? Here we come up against an impenetrable mystery.

What sort of existence has the soul when separated from the body? Does it possess a higher life, a fuller reality, in contrast to the earthly world around us (which nevertheless is also for us the quintessence of reality)?

Even the Church as we know it remains behind

Our inability to imagine the reality of the world beyond is all the more mysterious and fearful because all of earthly reality continues to exist and to march on. This is true not only of external things of no great importance, but also of all significant, important, and worthwhile things, above all of beloved persons. This is true of our entire civilization, of mankind's history with its points of progress and regression. This is true even of the Holy Church: it goes on — with its hierarchy, with the life of grace in souls, with all kinds of spiritual struggles and conversions. All these things continue to exist, while the person who dies is taken to a completely unknown country, with a mode of existence that we cannot even imagine.

Eternity is truly the goal, the *status finalis*, which alone can explain earthly life and earthly existence. And it is the Holy Church which tells us about eternity. Her very reason to exist stands or falls with the reality of eternity, with the continued existence of the human soul, with the glory of the kingdom of Heaven. But the Church directly accessible to us is the Church Militant, whose varied activities — even the streams of grace it constantly directs into the souls of the faithful — all take place within the sphere of earthly reality. The Church, of course, is not of this world. But it exists and acts in the earthly realm. It moves with mankind in *status viae*.

Considerations such as these suggest the mystery and dread of death as these emerge from the purely natural point of view. We become acutely aware of what we leave behind. We become equally aware that everything else goes on, that the earthly world continues to exist. From a purely natural perspective, this earthly reality is experienced as the fully real thing: death appears as that mysterious force which tears our person away from this fully real existence.

Death remains a dark and puzzling misfortune no matter how strongly we are convinced by rational arguments that the soul is immortal and no matter how much this conviction has changed our lives. Our rational certainty about life after death may indeed remove our terror over the meaninglessness of earthly life. But it can go no farther.

We continue to live in the shadow of death, soon to be separated by death from all the blessings of life which uplift us and are the source of great happiness for us. We also know that death will separate us from the one person we love above all else. We do not understand this separation. Death seems to us a total disaster, a pure evil.

Let us close our consideration of the natural face of death with the words of the *Preface* in the *Requiem Mass* of the Tridentine Liturgy, "*Ut, quos contristat certa moriendi conditio, eosdem consoletur futurae immortalitatis promissio*":

> In Christ the hope of a blessed resurrection
> has dawned for us, bringing all who are
> under the certain, sad sentence of death
> the consoling promise of future immortality.

Part II

Death in the light of Christian faith

IX

Our life as a pilgrimage

FOR Christians, earthly life is a pilgrimage. Not only do the great and significant things of earth contain hints of an unknown eternity; our whole life here below is a preparation for eternity, a pilgrimage toward our true, blessed home. St. Paul says that we are here on earth "awaiting our blessed hope."[50]

Eternal bliss is incomparably more important than all earthly happiness. The very reason for our existence is to be transformed in Christ and, thus, to glorify God. Because this transformation must be accomplished on earth, our life here is of great importance. Earthly life is a *status viae* — a pilgrimage. It reveals its importance only when we see it in its subordination to the *status finalis,* our true and final goal: eternal union with God, the Beatific Vision which brings us bliss without end.

I have already mentioned the *coincidentia oppositorum* — the situation in certain realms of being where at first glance two

---

[50] Tit. 2:13.

different aspects of a thing seem contradictory, but are then understood on a deeper level as complementing each other fully. Such is the case here. On the one hand, earthly life is grasped as being of decisive importance, for it is here on earth that our transformation has to be accomplished. On the other hand, earthly life would have no meaning if there were no eternity, if the goal did not lie at the end of the pilgrimage. No doubt our main emphasis must be on the goal, our blessed life in eternity; but we may not therefore deprive the pilgrimage of its decisive importance. It is rather the case that eternity increases the importance of the earthly life and makes it even more meaningful and charged with dramatic interest.

The Psalmist says, "In Thy light we see light."[51] For the Christian this is specifically the light of Christ. This illuminates everything for us. In it we see the true meaning and beauty of all natural blessings. When we read in the last book of the Bible, "Behold, I make all things new!,"[52] we are certainly entitled to apply this to the way in which we see all great blessings. They have become new and different as a direct result of Christ, the Incarnation, the Sacrifice on Calvary, and the Resurrection. Their true natural value and their great mystery have been enhanced, illuminated now by the light of Christ.

We have also a new awareness of moral wickedness: the dreadfulness of sin (which is an insult to God) and also the basic evil of indifference to God and even hatred of Him. The light of Christ illumines our true future, based on the great and frightful choice between obedience to God and rebellion, between Heaven and Hell.

[51] Ps. 35:10.
[52] Rev. 21:5.

X

Death as the hour of our judgment
— death's first supernatural aspect

DEATH assumes a new countenance in this light, and a doubly new aspect. Now it becomes the moment of judgment when we stand alone before the Divine Judge. Second, it becomes the moment of our face-to-face meeting with Jesus. The first inspires a reverent fear in us; the second, hope. In that masterful poem from the Middle Ages, the *Dies Irae* (so perfectly tuned to the theme of all *Requiem Masses*, where it finds a sublime place in the *Sequence*), stanzas emphasize now one, now the other aspect of death for Christians:

> *Quid sum miser tunc dicturus?*
> *Quem patronum rogaturus,*
> *Cum vix justus sit securus?*[53]

---

[53] *Dies Irae*, stanza 7.

69

> Wretched man, what can I plead?
> Whom to ask to intercede,
> When the just much mercy need?

These lines reveal a heart filled with reverent fear and awe before the majestic throne of Justice. Yet, in the next stanza, we pray with a heart filled with hope:

> *Rex tremendae majestatis,*
> *Qui salvandos salvas gratis,*
> *Salva me, fons pietatis.*

> Thou, O awe-inspiring Lord,
> Saving, e'en when unimplored,
> Save me, mercy's fount adored.

These two very contrasting attitudes of fear and hope are closely intertwined, complementing each other to establish the fully adequate response of the Christian to death. But because each aspect has its own, very different identity, I must now treat of each separately.

Christian fear of death as the moment of judgment

Let us first consider death as the moment of judgment. I do not speak here of the universal judgment, the Last Judgment at the end of the world, about which the *Dies Irae* sings with such moving power. I speak instead of the *personal* judgment of each individual soul, not yet related to the resurrection of the dead which is part of the Last Judgment. The eternal fate of each of us will be decided in that awesome moment of personal judgment when our soul stands before God.

As long as we were considering death merely from the natural point of view, our emphasis was on dread of it. I have already dealt with this obscure, puzzling aspect of death: the sudden, meaningless discontinuance of our earthly life, the anxiety underlying it as we face a going down into nothingness.

The Christian, supernatural point of view is fundamentally different. Here we encounter the tremendous seriousness of death as the moment when the very God who created us now calls us home and we have to give Him an accounting. No longer are we in the dark shadows of death. We stand instead before the great verdict. We shall hear from God either the horrifying doom of our condemnation to Hell or else a blissful invitation for us to enter the mansions of Heaven — even if this blissful moment is delayed by our stay in Purgatory.

Thus, death for the Christian consciousness no longer signifies a puzzling, fearful darkness. Rather it is a meaningful transition. In a certain sense, it is *the decisive event* of our life. Death signifies for the Christian the final seriousness of the time of judgment, not the dreadfully obscure, unimaginable and indefinite plunge into an inscrutable darkness.

A world of difference separates our *natural fear* of death (our anxieties about going into something completely unknown, our fear even about our own possible extinction) from the *holy fear* we have of the moment of God's judging us.[54]

---

[54] Fear of the judgment differs from that fear of the Lord which is mentioned in Psalm 111:10: "The fear of the Lord is the beginning of wisdom." For *fear of the Lord* refers to our response to God, to His infinite majesty, to the *mysterium tremendum* (the fearful mystery of God). This fear of the Lord can perfectly coexist with love; it will remain with us even as we partake of the bliss of the Beatific Vision. It must even be an ingredient of our reverent, loving response to the great God, the Mystery of Mysteries.

Christian hope in God's mercy

The way in which fear and hope coexist in our consciousness is a mystery; nevertheless, our holy fear of judgment must not be separated from our hope for eternal bliss.

On the one hand, we are aware that we are to appear before God, the absolute judge of our entire earthly life. This is the same God of which Holy Scripture says: "It is a fearful thing to fall into the hands of the living God."[55] This passage reminds us of the response we must make to the judgment. For our fear of the judgment must include also our fear of the punishment of Hell and, above all, our fear of eternal separation from God. This salutary fear is a value-response on our part.

On the other hand, it would be a false response — or more exactly, a response to a false image of God — if this fear of judgment were not accompanied by hope in God's mercy.

In the supernatural view, therefore, death is something to be feared as the moment of judgment. But because death also means our meeting with God's infinite mercy and with our Holy Redeemer, Jesus Christ (who has opened for us the gates of Heaven), death must also fill us with the greatest hope. Hope ought even to have a certain advantage over fear: "In Thee, O Lord, have I hoped. Let me never be confounded."[56]

---

[55] Heb. 10:31.

[56] Conclusion of the Ambrosian song of praise, *Te Deum*: "*In te Domine speravi, non confundar in aeternum.*"

XI

Death as union with Jesus
— death's second supernatural aspect

WE come now to the second supernatural aspect of death: our meeting with Jesus. St. Thomas Aquinas gives beautiful expression to this in his hymn, *Adoro Te Devote*:

> *Jesu, quem velatum nunc aspicio,*
> *Oro, fiat illud, quod tam sitio:*
> *Ut, te revelata cernens facie,*
> *Visu sim beatus tuae gloriae.*

> Jesus! Whom for the present veil'd I see,
> What I so thirst for, O, vouchsafe to me:
> That I may see Thy countenance unfolding,
> And may be blest Thy glory in beholding.

My emphasis on death as our final union with Jesus, the God-Man, should in no way be interpreted as meaning that the Beatific Vision does not consist primarily in seeing God the

Father, nay, the Most Holy Trinity. Let us recall the words of Christ to Philip: "Have I been with you so long, Philip, and yet you do not know me? I tell you, he who sees me sees the Father."[57] Even while Christ was on earth, His sacred humanity somehow revealed the Father.

But this epiphany of God in Jesus's humanity will be far surpassed in the Beatific Vision by the direct vision of God: the Father, the Son, and the Holy Spirit.

Therefore, we must clearly distinguish our *direct* vision of God (after our death) from our knowledge of Him through the humanity of Christ. The *Preface* of the *Christmas Mass* gives an admirable expression of the relation between Christ's sacred humanity and the revelation to us of the Father: "By the mystery of the Word made flesh, from Thy brightness a new light has risen to shine upon the eyes of our souls, in order that, God becoming visible to us, we may be borne upwards to the love of things invisible."

The scope of this work requires me to limit myself to just a few words about the Beatific Vision, our unique union in eternity with the God-Man, Jesus Christ. The Liturgy often refers to this union, as in the following passage from *Ubi caritas*[58]:

> *Simul quoque cum Beatis videamus.*
> *Glorianter vultum tuum, Christe Deus:*
> *Gaudium, quod est immensum atque probum,*
> *Saecula per infinita saeculorum.*

---

[57] John 14:9.

[58] Conclusion of the antiphon *Ubi caritas*, which was sung at the washing of the feet ceremony on Holy Thursday.

Let us also with the blessed see
Thy face in glory, O Christ our God,
There to possess immeasurable and happy joy
For infinite ages and ages.

Death unites the saved with those who are in Heaven

From this most intimate union with God arises also a transfigured union with all who are in Heaven. Thus, the Catholic
prayers for the burial of a faithful one include this antiphon:

In paradisum deducant te Angeli:
In tuo adventu suscipiant te Martyres,
Et perducant te in civitatem sanctam Jerusalem.

May the angels lead you into Paradise;
May the martyrs welcome you on your arrival
And bring you into the holy city of Jerusalem.

In the Propers of many masses for the saints, we find reference made to this joyous communion. Thus, for example, the
Gradual for the feast of St. Martin of Tours speaks of "one whom
the angels and archangels have welcomed." The Gradual for the
feast of St. Francis of Assisi contains these words: "The poor and
humble Francis enters Heaven as a rich man, and is welcomed
with heavenly songs."

It is obvious that our eternal bliss includes also this communion of saints. The Beatific Vision which the blessed shall have
of God — a fulfillment that surpasses all understanding — includes also the highest fulfillment of all human communities.
We are united in a profound way with all other souls who have
attained eternal bliss. In a special way, this involves the final

fulfillment of our relationship with those we have most loved on earth.

The Christian view of death, therefore, reveals that through death we enter into a unique communion with all those who are in Heaven, especially with those deeply loved persons who have died before us. Even so, this view of death as gateway to eternal bliss does not take away the solitude of dying — a condition which is surely related to our earthly situation.

But the solitude is not unlimited. We who are yet alive on earth continue to love the departed persons; we also continue to think of their present existence in eternity. True enough that our direct contact with our beloved dead has ceased, but our deeply spiritual communion goes on. We can invoke the dead. In faith we can assume that in eternity they know about us, and that, despite their new form of existence which is quite unknown to us, we nevertheless can reach them with the voice of our hearts. In his *Sermon 26* on the *Song of Solomon*, St. Bernard laments his brother's death but affirms: "You will never forget me."[59] Death remains a uniquely solitary experience, but for Christians our dreadful farewell is immersed in our hope for a blessed reunion in eternity.

[59] Cf. Ps. 13:1.

XII

The meaning Christ gives to death

I WILL explore further the glorious, supernatural aspect of death revealed through Christian faith. But first I must refer once more to the fundamental difference between the natural aspect (which contains no real insight into the immortality of the soul) and the supernatural aspect (which focuses upon death as the moment of judgment). The natural aspect shows death to be something puzzling, obscure, meaningless. The supernatural aspect, rooted in faith, shows death as implying the greatness of our human destiny and eternal fate. This reference to our *status finalis* points to the deep significance of a human life: we reap in eternity what we have sown on earth. The moment of death is something awesome, mixing as it does our hope for heavenly bliss with our fear of Hell.

In both views of death the manner of our existence after death remains an unimaginable mystery. But the supernatural view, bathed in the light of Christian revelation, shows that a decisive event awaits each of us after death: judgment. The breathtaking alternatives at stake here — Heaven or Hell —

are not found in the same way in any merely rational certainty about the soul's immortality.

To be sure, such a rational certainty does include some concept of a judgment made by God on our earthly life. This is clear from Plato's myth in the *Gorgias* and also in the *Republic*.[60] Nevertheless, there is a decisive difference between the view of God's judgment afforded by Christian revelation, and the expectation, based on belief in the immortality of the soul, of God's judgment after death. In both the *Phaedo* and the *Apology*, Socrates makes splendid comments about the soul, but the judgment that is to come is seldom in the foreground. In the framework of a rationally understood immortality, there is no consciousness of sin as an offense against a personal God.[61]

For Socrates, of course, God is recognized as the judge of what is morally wrong. But a person such as Socrates could know nothing about the new relationship of men with a personal God who is offended by sin. The purely rational concept of God is incomparably more vague than the *living* and *seeing* God of the Old Testament and, above all, of the New Testament.

The Christian's constant awareness of death

The natural awareness of immortality is far removed from the powerful, meaningful, "existential" view of death found in

[60] Plato, *Gorgias* 523A-527E; *The Republic* 614A-616A.

[61] Sören Kierkegaard has brilliantly defended this point in a number of places. For example, "The concept of guilt and sin does not in the deepest sense emerge in paganism." Sören Kierkegaard, *The Concept of Dread*, III, 2 (Princeton: Princeton University Press, 1957), 87; and "The Socratic Definition of Sin" in *Sickness Unto Death*, II, 2 (Princeton: Princeton University Press, 1980).

the *Dies Irae*. In the totally supernatural perspective of this sacred poem, the truth that *we live out our lives in the shadow of death* takes on a new character. For we realize that we do not know when the hour of God's judgment will come; we do not know when we shall be summoned before the Divine Judge on that "day of wrath." The somber words of Christ enforce the supernatural realization of the meaning of death: "And you also must be prepared, for the Son of Man shall come at an hour you do not expect." [62]

The Christian awareness of death does not generate the kind of uncertainty which might cause us to ask, "Is my final hour on earth coming tomorrow?" Instead, it moves us to be prepared for God's awesome appearance at the end of our lives. This Christian expectation of death prevents our being ensnared by the illusion that, since we feel ourselves to be healthy and sound, death is a long way off. It also prevents our being crippled by a paralyzing anxiety that, since there is no certainty in life, death might snatch us away at any minute.

This awareness conforms to man's true metaphysical situation. Our eyes are raised to God. We live in His presence. We experience a holy fear which is organically linked to our effort to make good use of the time remaining to us, even as St. Paul says to "make the most of the time."[63]

Death consummates our longed-for union with Jesus

Death presents still a new countenance for those who, loving Jesus with a profound and ultimate love, are consumed with longing for a face-to-face union with Him, and with the Father

[62] Lk. 12:40.
[63] Eph. 5:16.

in and through Him. This aspect of death is expressed by the customary exclamation in many cloisters as the hour of death tolls for a member of their monastic community: "Behold, the Bridegroom cometh! Go forth to meet Him!"[64]

The aspect of death as the moment of judgment has not disappeared, but the union with Jesus is now in the foreground. There is here no false certainty. No religious sense of optimism thrusts aside the seriousness of the great judgment. But the wishful longing and hoping for Jesus, the tempestuous and impatient yearning for the Beloved, are dominant. To see death thus as the fulfillment of our union in love has nothing in common with giddy enthusiasm. The holy sobriety of a soul filled with the light of Christ is joined to the victorious intoxication of love.

We can recognize in the life of any given saint various periods: times of great aridity are followed by times of mystical grace. In a similar way, there are times when the thought of death causes our heart to tremble, such as when we think of the hour of judgment. At other times, the thought of death brings with it an ardent longing for the eternal union in love with Jesus. Both attitudes can even exist simultaneously in the soul in such a way that the blissful aspect — which is deeply tied to hope — is dominant.

[64] Mt. 25:6.

XIII

Christian hope

TO GRASP this, we must consider hope in general, and then come to understand its significance in the relationship of Christians to eternity.

First, we must distinguish hope from all apparently similar attitudes (such as expectation and desire) and then distinguish between the hope of a nonbeliever and that of a Christian. Finally, we must distinguish *natural hope* from *supernatural hope*, the latter being one of the three theological virtues.

The nature of hope

Hope is one of those basic attitudes without which human life would be unendurable, even impossible. I refer here to an attitude adopted in certain situations when we are faced with the uncertain outcome of an undertaking. In such situations, we hope for a favorable outcome even if all reasonable calculations are against it. This is especially the case when we are threatened with a great misfortune or when we are gravely concerned over the serious illness of someone we love. Despite our slim chances of escaping the misfortune in the first instance or of recovery in the second, we still feel hope.

Whenever he feels hope, even an atheist — or at least someone who reckons himself an atheist — is counting on the intervention of an all-good, all-powerful Being. Hope can exist even when misfortune seems inevitable according to the normal rules of cause and effect.

Hope is one of those basic human attitudes in which we see our primordial link with God — our undeniable metaphysical situation of creaturehood and our total dependence on God — win acceptance over all theories and opinions. We may speak and sometimes even think like an atheist, but in times of great danger we rely on the power and benevolence of God to save us. Our earthly life would be unendurable if we lacked this kind of hope — unless a deceptive form of optimism took its place.

Optimism differs from hope

The purely human form of optimism must be sharply distinguished even from the natural hope which we have been discussing. Optimists are like certain weighted toys: they always land on their feet when they fall down. People with hope, on the contrary, become more aware of things; their spirits rise when they break through the boundaries and limits in which they have enclosed themselves. A faint light rises to illumine everything taking place. Hope is a specifically spiritual attitude, an awakening in the face of great trials.

On the other hand, the human optimism that carries us through trials is based on a great illusion. It is not a spiritual attitude but a result of one's temperament; it is blind to the metaphysical situation of mankind.

People filled with genuine hope become more attractive by reason of that hope. Seeing them moves us, whereas those filled with a merely vital optimism (arising from their temperament) do not impress us at all. They definitely do not become more attractive but, rather, they cause in us a certain amount of amusement.

Through hope, persons become more objective; they tower over the subjective world around them. Through mere human optimism, they become subjective: they misinterpret reality and become victims of their own merely human tendencies and desires.[65]

Christian hope includes a value-response to God

Natural hope, already something noble, takes on another characteristic for a Christian. Christian hope does not, like natural hope, merely presuppose silently and objectively the Providence of a loving God.[66] It is based, above all, on a conscious, express response to a merciful God who has revealed himself to us in Jesus Christ.

This supernatural hope is most closely tied to prayers of petition which we address to an almighty, infinitely good God.

---

[65] Appendix B considers natural hope in greater detail, and discusses the differences between hope, expectation, desire, willing, and wishing.

[66] The limits of this present work make it impossible to elaborate a detailed distinction between a hope that only tacitly presupposes God and a hope based on a conscious belief in the God of Christian Revelation. I have referred to this well-known distinction in more than one of my previous works in which I distinguished the Christian (or supernatural) form of morality from purely natural morality. Cf. the final chapter in each of the following books: *Ethics*, *Situation Ethics*, and *Graven Images*.

We beg God to grant us the happy outcome of an event of great concern to us, or we beg Him to prevent some awful misfortune.

In other words, hope *always* contains a value-response. Even though its formal object is *what is objectively good for me*, hope is also a response to God's infinite goodness and to His loving-kindness.

Right here lies the decisive difference between hope and all wishing and expectation. There is no value-response in expectation. The certainty that something will happen is a purely *theoretical* response, somehow rooted in our knowledge. Wishing, too, though it may be an *affective* response, is yet not necessarily a value-response.

We may hope for some outcome which is not only a great benefit to ourselves but also associated with important values, with things which are good quite independent of any good bestowed on us. This is also the case with wishing: we may wish for the success of some important enterprise just because it is good, and not because it confers any benefit on us.

But in this present analysis of hope as a value-response, I am not concerned with what might be called the *formal object* of some response, whether hoping or wishing or willing. I refer rather to hope as a response to God's loving-kindness. Like a prayer of petition, hope responds to the infinite goodness of God.

The value-response in hope is, therefore, unique, for it is not addressed to the value of some desired goal. It is addressed rather to God, the basis of hope, the Reality who makes hope meaningful and possible. Hope thus has quite a different relationship to value than the one we find in reverence, love, or adoration. The relationship in hope is our counting on the infinite loving-kindness and almighty power of God. We have confidence and faith in these divine attributes. Thus, we touch now upon the close ties between faith and hope, a topic to which I shall return later in some detail.[67]

Christian hope is directed to our union with Jesus

The theological virtue of hope is directed toward an eternal, blissful union with Jesus and — in and through Him — with God the Father. This supernatural hope deeply modifies a Christian believer's view of death.

Eternal bliss is the highest objective benefit for a human being. This benefit presupposes an ultimate and ardent love of Christ and of God in and through Christ. The eternal, indestructible union of love with Jesus precisely constitutes the Beatific Vision, and it would not be beatific if we did not love God above all else.

Our hope of eternal bliss, therefore, presupposes the value-response of love for God. God himself desires this highest good for humanity and has intended us for it. If, through our own fault, we forfeit this good, this must be in God's eyes, too, a great misfortune.

When our concerns center around earthly benefits or misfortunes — hopes for the greatest good thing or the prevention of the most dreadful kind of misfortune — our prayers should always end with the qualification, "Yet, not my will be done, O Lord, but Thine!"[68] Our hope that God may grant us

---

[67] Besides the difference between natural and supernatural hope, which I have already briefly sketched, there is another distinction to be made, which concerns the kinds of things that might be hoped for, the *formal objects* of our hope. Appendix C discusses these differences.

[68] Luke 22:42.

the good thing or avert the misfortune is also the basis of the act whereby we surrender totally to God's will.

When, however, our hope concerns our eternal salvation, it makes no sense to pray, "Lord, grant me eternal bliss; yet, let not my will be done, but Thine." The point here is not that we are certain that we can pass safely though the judgment when we stand before God. We are in fact uncertain. It may be that we shall forfeit eternal union with God because of our sins. Yet this lack of certainty about our own salvation in no way is equivalent to praying, when it comes to our own salvation, "Not my will be done, O Lord, but Thine!"

We cannot doubt that God wants us to long for eternal bliss with all our heart. Not to do so would be a dreadful sin. Only through our sins — offenses against God — can we forfeit our eternal bliss.

In this context we must see that the thought that we might renounce our own eternal salvation for the sake of someone else necessarily leads to an absurdity. When St. Paul exclaims that he is willing to be damned if this would effect the conversion and salvation of his blood-brothers, the Jews, we must see this as a moving expression of his love for them. But such a renunciation, taken literally, is strictly impossible. There can be no trade-off here between some good for me which I renounce so as to procure some greater good for my brothers. At stake now is eternal salvation. The only way I can lose this, in contrast to any natural good, is through sin. It is absurd to imagine that God would "reward" with the eternal punishment of Hell the almost excessive generosity of a person who loves others with such unselfish devotion.

No, our hope of eternal salvation presupposes not only the loving value-response to God; it also presupposes an awareness of the infinite, objective value of our eternal beatitude which

God wills, and which itself both presupposes and includes the glorification of God which takes place through us. We then can see that hope in our eternal beatitude differs from the hope directed toward all other beneficial goods for us. Moreover, we see its incomparable value because it is rooted in the highest, the most fundamental value-response: the love of God and the love of neighbor.

XIV

Christ transforms death

CHRISTIAN hope places a completely different character on the face of death. For death becomes now the hour of our encounter with the Holy of Holies, Jesus Christ, in whose heart the fullness of the Godhead dwells. Death means the encounter at last with the God-Man, the Beloved of our soul, the One for whom we have been created.

As I have already stated, supernatural hope presupposes our ultimate love for Jesus and, in and through Him, for the Father. This love, too, plays its role in the new character which death assumes for the Christian. It is because we love God that death is the culmination of our life, the beginning of our true and eternal life. Love is the necessary precondition for our longing for the Beatific Vision as the summit of eternal happiness. Love turns the fearful, sinister death which threatens us — the shadow of death — into a blessed moment in which we are called to eternal life.

In the light of Christ's revelation, death takes on a completely new appearance: in Christ, in His teachings, and in His promises, the meaning for our existence shines forth clearly. We grasp that life on earth is a pilgrimage and life after death a blessed fulfillment. The light of Christ illuminates the darkness of death.

Without Christ's revelation, death could never appear in this unique light as our moment of fulfillment and we could never hope for an eternal union of love with God. Never could this ultimate love of God blossom within us without the Incarnation, without the epiphany of God in the sacred humanity of Jesus. Indeed, without the sacrament of Baptism and the infusion of salvific grace into our souls, supernatural love could not develop within us.

Only through the light of Christ can death lose its dread and become the hour of the soul's marriage with its beloved Jesus. But for this to be realized, our soul must give the response of faith to Christ and to His Revelation. To the degree, therefore, that our faith, hope, and love increase, the natural view of death — with its night of fear — will give way to the view of death as gateway to a blissful union with Jesus Christ.[69]

The relation between death's two supernatural aspects

I have said that the supernatural view of death includes two different aspects: it is seen as both the hour of our judgment and of our blissful meeting with the Bridegroom. Both aspects somehow coexist in the lives of saints. One aspect may be stressed over the other, but no one of them can ever be totally absent. Which aspect has the greater prominence depends above all on

---

[69] I shall give a more detailed analysis of this point later on, when I discuss the great task every Christian has to replace the natural with the supernatural view of death.

God — whether He wishes to test some soul through a night of holy fear or whether He wishes a blissful hope to bloom in the soul. Thus, when Hugh of St. Victor was dying, he is reported to have expressed his gratitude to God for the infinite grace of an imminent death filled with the most profound joy and vivid sense of longing. Such a death is a special grace from God.

The same blissful aspect of death can also be revealed in other ways. Thus, those present at the death of the great French Oratorian, Alphonse Gratry, reported their unmistakable feeling that a sun was sinking below the horizon as he died. Access to a person's soul after death is denied us, not because the soul has ceased to exist but because we can no longer perceive it in the body left behind.

The relationship of the two supernatural aspects of death to one another is very different from the relationship of each one to the natural aspect of death. Rational certainty about the immortality of the soul (attained from the natural aspect of death) serves as a preamble to Christian certainty about immortality (which is based on faith and hope in Christ). The natural certainty (or, in many respects, the anxious concern about immortality) is transfigured by Christian faith into an existential reality that is constantly before our eyes.

I shall never forget the exclamations of my friend, the great philosopher Adolf Reinach, before he became a Christian: "Death is the most important moment in life! Dying is life's most important act!" Reinach was an ardent admirer of Plato's *Phaedo* and we might be tempted to say that he was but paraphrasing Socrates. But Reinach was a thinker so focused on truth that the "words of the master" would never have moved him to make such an exclamation had he not grasped the illuminating truth himself. Through the force of reason alone he somehow understood that death is the beginning of our true life, a transition to our *status finalis*. But, lacking faith at the time, he did not see death as either the hour of judgment or of our blissful union with Jesus.[70]

This example of Reinach clearly displays the difference between the supernatural view of death afforded by the light of Christ, and the view afforded by rational certainty about the immortality of the soul. The light of Christ differs enormously from the noble, but far dimmer, clarity which true metaphysics diffuses.

And hope in Christ likewise differs greatly from the natural *sursum corda* — the "lift up your hearts!" — which we find in those enlightened by reason alone. Faith sheds upon us the light of Christ, and this reveals the Sun of Justice and the irresistible attractiveness of the One "who has called you out of darkness into His marvelous light."[71]

Death's natural and supernatural aspects compared

Another difference now requires our attention: the difference between the supernatural view of death and an apparently natural aspect of death that we might call *naive* — a view which looks upon death as something to be dreaded.

Specifically, how far should the view of death in the light of Christian belief replace the naive view of death as something to be dreaded? Should death's fearful aspect be completely eliminated from the Christian consciousness? Or should it remain as something subordinate and partial, to be transcended victoriously by the Christian aspect?

[70] During World War I he found faith in Christ. A short time later, on November 16, 1917, he died on the battlefield.

[71] 1 Pet. 2:9.

Let us recall the warning the Church gives the faithful on Ash Wednesday when the priest marks our forehead with a cross of ashes: "Remember, man, you are dust and unto dust you shall return!" This dramatically shows the Church's insistence that although the Christian view of death (which indeed is death's only true estimate) must be the definitive perspective for us, nonetheless the natural view with all its dread should not disappear totally from our consciousness.

Eternal rest and perpetual light in death

That the Church's Liturgy is aimed at the various aspects of death is but another sign of the greatness, truthfulness, and classical character of the Liturgy. The *Requiem* prayer *"Requiem aeternam dona ei Domine"* ("Grant eternal rest, O Lord, unto Thy servant") emphasizes not only the prayer that the departed soul be saved from eternal damnation, but also that there be a cessation of all sorrows to which humans are subject on their pilgrimage through this valley of tears.

If the Church ended her prayer for the dead with just this part, the situation would be unsatisfactory and even very upsetting. But the prayer continues, "...*et lux perpetua luceat ei*" ("...and let perpetual light shine upon him"). This now includes reference to the person's existing in an eternity filled with the highest and most unimaginable conscious awareness. It also illumines the true meaning of *eternal rest* spoken in the first part of the prayer. Because of the second part (with its reference to *perpetual light*), there can be no misunderstanding of death as a mere cessation of all sufferings, as a mere end to strife and profound cares. The word *rest* seems to emphasize death as just such a cessation, upon the analogy of a peaceful sleep. But this affords a view only of the negative side of death.

Granted that it is a great gift, the cessation of all suffering and worries is still not bliss in any positive sense. We can see this in earthly experience: the happiness that comes from being cured of a serious illness is very different from the purely positive gift from God of rejoicing in a great love for another person. Thus, in the *Requiem* prayer, *perpetual light* points to the positive bliss of the departed soul, even as *rest* points to the end of suffering in the sleep of death.

Both views need to be expressed. With admirable realism the Church takes each into account. The cessation of all suffering is necessarily a part of eternal bliss, for "God will wipe away every tear."[72] These heartening words point to eternal life as precisely differing from life in this valley of tears.

The expression *sleep of peace* highlights another quality in the supernatural aspect of death, namely, that it marks a *redemption*, a harmonious state of being. Not *sleep* but, rather, *peace* is emphasized here, and this in a positive sense. For *peace* in a religious sense signifies not only the absence of all division and strife but also a heartwarming positive presence. Thus, the peace of Christ shines forth in a positive way when Christ greets the Apostles with the words, "Peace be with you."[73] So, too, we say at every Mass, "Grant us peace."

The same spirit is found in the Franciscan greeting, *"Pax et bonum!"* ("Peace and salvation!") The peace of Christ contains the sweetness of our union with God and it is an element of eternal bliss.

The essence of the Redemption includes both the cessation of what is negative and the attainment of what is purely positive. The Redemption is primarily a liberation from our frightful

[72] Rev. 7:17; 21:4.
[73] Luke 24:36.

separation from God. It contains our reconciliation with Him. Were it not for Original Sin and the countless actual sins committed on earth, no redemption would be necessary. The Redemption cleanses us from our sins, frees us from the chains of sin, and brings about our rebirth as new creatures in Christ.

Above all, however, the Redemption saves us from eternal damnation: it bestows salvation on us. We humans were incapable of salvation for so long as our race was chained in sin. But Christ's Redemption shatters the chains and opens for us the door to eternal bliss. The mystery of this Redemption is clearly inexhaustible. This one single word conceals a world of bliss. A product of the divine mercy, the Redemption is deeply linked to the mysteries of the Incarnation and of Christ's Sacrifice on the Cross. In the Redemption, we find liberation from all evils, the expunging of all guilt, and, above all, the illumination of eternal bliss.

Death as our true awakening

The supernatural view of death in a certain sense sees our earthly existence as a *being asleep*, and considers death to be the beginning of our awakening. Death begins a mode of existence for our personal being which has an intensity and awareness beyond our ability to imagine.

Death begins that incomprehensible bliss of eternal union with Jesus which is suggested by St. Thomas Aquinas in his hymn, *Adoro Te Devote*:

> *Jesu, quem velatum nunc aspicio,*
> *Oro, fiat illud, quod tam sitio:*
> *Ut, te revelata cernens facie,*
> *Visu sim beatus tuae gloriae.*

> Jesus! Whom for the present veil'd I see,
> What I so thirst for, O, vouchsafe to me:
> That I may see Thy countenance unfolding,
> And may be blest Thy glory in beholding.

Similarly, St. Teresa of Avila, in speaking of an advanced stage of mystical experience, compares its extraordinary ecstasy (which she describes as an elevation into Heaven) with death (that is to say, with the bliss we hope to attain after death).

The transiency of life and the rhythm of decay

Earlier, we witnessed a mysterious contradiction inherent in the natural aspect of death. We must return to this feature in examining the relationship existing between the fearful natural aspect of death and the supernatural aspect: on the one hand, we experience the transiency and impermanence of earthly things and, on the other, the hint or promise of an incomparably better world, a world of completion and fulfillment.

There is a bitter French adage which expresses the transiency of life and all earthly things, including the most touching and beautiful: *"Tout lasse, tout casse, tout passe; il n'y a que le souvenir qui reste."* ("Everything declines, everything shatters, everything passes, and only memories remain.") This is a grim truth, never to be minimized or forgotten. At the same time, however, the very earthly experiences which move us to repeat the adage carry with them the hint and the promise mentioned above.

I speak here of experiences involving all great values: sublime beauty, deep loves, and above all, the transcendent splendor of true morality. All these shine forth with a promise of intransiency — of permanence.

Goethe rightly says of the blissful glance of mutual love that it must be eternal; otherwise it would be nothing.[74]

The human heart has an ambivalent attitude toward change and permanence. On the one hand, we seem to require change. If we cling always to one and the same old thing, we become indifferent to its value. We long for change and we feel the attraction of what is new and unknown. On the other hand, we also experience the tragedy of impermanence. We see change as something deeply painful. We think that only a superficial person would look upon change as attractive or desirable. Change is life's tragedy just as the bitter adage expresses it.

Complaints about change and impermanence often flow from sad experiences of life. How many lovers are there whose loved ones have proven unfaithful! How many serious promises have been broken by the fickleness of the human heart! How often does a change in circumstances cause something to lose its high value for us! How many good plans come to nothing; how many once promising conversions fail to be fulfilled!

We must see that many things are of their very nature unchangeable. In and of themselves, in their essence, values such as justice and kindliness cannot change; nor can the beauty of purity, the moving sublimity of trust and generosity. These bear within themselves the promise of an eternal existence which awaits us. Not only moral values but also the great beauty of art and nature, metaphysical truth, and, above all,

---

[74] Cf. *Faust*, pt. 1, lines 3188-92: "*...Laß diesen Blick,/ Laß diesen Händedruck dir sagen,/ Was unaussprechlich ist./ Sich hinzugeben ganz und eine Wonne/ Zu fühlen, die ewig sein muß!*" ("Let this gaze,/ This pressure of my hands express to you/ What is ineffable:/ To give one's whole soul and feel/ An ecstasy that must endure forever!") Johann Wolfgang von Goethe, *Faust: A Tragedy*, trans. Walter Arndt, ed. Cyrus Hamlin (New York: W. W. Norton & Company, 1976), 78.

love: all these are permanent in their nature and all point to a world beyond this earthly one.

But the *bearers* of these values can and do change. They are subject to the rhythm of inconstancy and decay. A good man can experience grave moral failure, can forfeit his virtue. A splendid landscape can be destroyed by natural forces or by industrial "progress." A magnificent palace, a fine church, or a wonderful piece of sculpture can be destroyed. A painting of peerless beauty can go up in flames. This rhythm of decay permeates all the known world and is especially evident in the relentless rhythm of life and death which dominates all living creatures on earth.

Our longing for permanence

A similar rhythm often reaches into the human heart and causes to fade away those attitudes whose very essence and meaning are such that they should remain constant.

But this is not inevitably the case with all hearts. Decay and inconstancy do belong to the very nature of natural living things and render inevitable the rhythm of life and death and endless change. Not so with certain human hearts: some are constant. They embody attitudes whose essences point to eternity. They are faithful all life long. There are promises that are never broken and loves that last until the dying breath of the lovers, that exhibit a moving and absolute fidelity.

During our lifetime, therefore, two contrasting melodies sound in our ear: the song of impermanence and the song of eternal duration. They contradict each other only when one of them makes an all-encompassing claim. Reality presents us with some things impermanent by nature but also with other things that ought to endure. No doubt everything in life fades away. This is not tragic in itself even if the process of fading away contains so many mysteries of a metaphysical nature. But there are other things which, although they can fade away, can and ought to endure. Something is wrong when they fail to endure.

Here we touch on the most profound aspect of our personal being: here the fading away becomes something tragic. There lives deep within the human soul a longing for the continuance of the soul, for eternal life. We seldom focus explicitly on the boundless benefit of personal existence, but at times it comes vividly before our minds. Like the peal of an organ, it echoes through our entire life.

Part of the tragic aspect of our earthly life centers precisely on the fading away of attitudes which can and should be constant. I am thinking here of our fidelity to God and to the persons for whom God has planted a deep love within our heart: how often have we ourselves allowed these to become faint, if not to fade altogether away! So, too, we witness a similar infidelity in others. Attitudes within them which should have endured forever come tragically to an end.

Even though their earthly bearers are all too changeable, the permanent things (such as metaphysical truths, moral values, and other values which are eternal as such) announce a message that contradicts the naive aspect of our own death, the death of all other human beings, and particularly, the death of those we deeply love.

Death's meaning as a punishment for sin

The light of Christ effects a radical change in the totality of our earthly life and, especially, in death. It changes also the two *songs* — of transiency and permanence.

In the light of divine Revelation, death, which often enough is linked with great physical suffering, is a punishment for Original Sin.[75] According to Christian teaching, in the Garden of Paradise there was to be no death, with all its terror, but rather a blessed, peaceful transition from the *status viae* to the *status finalis* — from pilgrimage to final goal.

Precisely because death is a punishment, it loses the note of meaninglessness that characterizes the fact that a lower element destroys something higher and much more precious. There is a deep meaning to suffering understood as a punishment from God: it reveals God's basic attitude toward human guilt. Thus, out of the bleakness of the inevitable rhythm taking place apart from and beyond everything of value, death is inexplicably brought into the bright light of the great, basic contrast between good and evil.

Death's meaning as the moment of our judgment

The natural aspect of death undergoes a second change as a result of faith, a change even greater than its being seen as a punishment for sin. For after death comes the great decision about our eternal destiny. The need to die is now our common human destiny. It is the punishment for Adam's sin.

Still more important, the judgment that awaits each of us after death decides whether or not we shall put on the festive garment of eternal, unbounded happiness. Did a given man die in the state of grace, in the basic attitude of knowing and loving God? Or did he sin against the light, reject God — and then die impenitent? The judgment of each individual leads either to

---

[75] St. Augustine, *The City of God*, 13.7.

eternal damnation or to eternal bliss. We therefore await it with both fear and hope.

From this perspective, death is not at all what it seems to be to a naive, natural consciousness. Death now sorts out what really matters. Now what matters is how we have lived our earthly life. What has deeply moved us here? What have we done here? What have we failed to do? The worthless things, of course, which appealed to us because of some pleasant feature, now sink into insignificance. This is especially true of all the worldly interests which smothered us in so many details.

The deep questions, however, remain. Did we give to God's commandments the responses we should have given? Did we long to be transformed in Christ? Have we really tried to live according to this viewpoint? All such matters now take on a true, extraordinary, and profoundly valid significance.

Many of us fail to understand the importance our conduct has in God's eyes. We don't take ourselves (and our conduct) seriously. We deem anthropocentric the idea that our lives possess a moral and religious significance important to God. Indeed, we may allege it to be incompatible with God's infinite majesty that He should even notice our conduct, much less be "bothered" with it.

But this is a fatal error, a blind, stupid attitude. St. Augustine exclaims that God is a *"Deus vivens et videns"* — "a living and a seeing God"[76] God is infinitely holy. According to St. John, "God is love."[77] God takes humanity seriously, so much so that He attributes the highest significance to the question of moral good and evil. God, who knows everything, knows everything about each of us. We can conceal nothing from His perfect gaze.

[76] St. Augustine, *Sermon* 69.3.
[77] 1 John 4:8.

Thus the Psalmist says, "Whither shall I go from Thy spirit? Or whither shall I flee from Thy face? If I ascend into heaven, Thou art there; and if I descend into Hell, Thou art there also!"[78] Christ has himself taught us that the very hairs on our head are numbered.[79]

God's incomprehensible greatness is expressed by His taking seriously the humanity created in His image. This greatness finds, as it were, its highest expression in the absolute significance God attributes to the conduct of human beings. We are endowed with free will; we are confronted with the conflict between good and evil, with the axis of the spiritual universe. We must indeed tremble before God's judgment as before something awesome and crucial.

But how dreadful would it be if there were no divine judgment, if God were indifferent to sin, indifferent to how we used our free will! Does not God's judgment show forth His infinite love in the ultimate seriousness with which He regards the depths of our soul?

All these considerations show us that the light of Revelation affords us a view of death far different from the naive and natural view. Dying now is seen, not as a fearful and mysterious going down into nothingness, but as a door opening to the *status finalis* and to the fulfillment of our deepest longings. In Jesus, the mercy of God is illuminated for us. The Church prays, *"Deus, qui omnipotentiam tuam parcendo maxime et miserando manifestas!"* ("O God! Thy almighty power is made most evident in Thy mercy and compassion!")[80]

---

[78] Ps. 139:7-8.
[79] Luke 12:7.
[80] Prayer in the Mass for the Tenth Sunday after Pentecost.

In accord with this prayer, that aspect of death which sees it as the door to eternal bliss should outshine all other considerations.

All Christians must strive to succeed in the great task of having this victorious aspect of death outshine the natural aspect of death's fearful inevitability. This latter view is a threat to death's glorious mission to allow the marriage of the soul with the Bridegroom. As we strive to make our own this supernatural view of death, our constant prayer must be: "May God grant us this grace — to be led by death to the Bridegroom!"

XV

Attaining the Christian view of death

THE STRENGTH of a man's faith determines the extent to which he will accept the glorious aspect of death. There are many degrees of faith: from a merely conventional faith (produced by the social environment, family, or national tradition) to a personal, living faith all the way to the unshakable faith of the saints. They have the victorious faith that can move mountains and that includes a total commitment of their spirit and an absolute certainty of conviction about the things of faith.

The necessity of cooperation with grace

Although faith is a grace given to us by God, it nonetheless demands great cooperation on our part. We must be ready to receive and to accept Revelation, and free to respond to it. "Blessed are they who have not seen, and yet have believed,"[81]

---

[81] John 20:29.

says Jesus to the Apostle Thomas. Here, *seeing* refers to the natural ascertaining of a fact, such as Thomas's actually touching the wounds of Christ in His hands and His side. In this sense, *seeing* in no way implies understanding God's epiphany in the sacred humanity of Jesus — an understanding which forced St. Peter to his knees and led him to exclaim, "Depart from me, O Lord, for I am a sinful man!"[82] Those whose faith is praised are the very persons who give the correct response to the sacred humanity which the *Preface* for Christmas mentions: "By the mystery of the Word made Flesh, a new ray of Thy glory has shone on the eyes of our mind; that, while we know our God visibly, we may be drawn upward to the love of things invisible."[83]

In our response to God's epiphany we have free choice. Many of us flee from grace. We shut our soul when God knocks. Others, however, freely surrender, open wide their souls to receive God's gift, and pray for an increase in faith. Faith demands cooperation on our part: "He who made thee without thee will not justify thee without thee." (*"Qui ergo fecit te sine te, non te justificat sine te."*)[84] These words of St. Augustine are applicable also to the gift of faith. It is freely offered to us in the first place but it will not take root, grow, and flourish without our own free cooperation. Thus, the very words of Christ point to our personal responsibility: "He who believes and is baptized

---

[82] Luke 5:8.

[83] *"Quia per incarnati Verbi mysterium nova mentis nostrae oculis lux tuae claritatis infulsit: ut, dum visibiliter Deum cognoscimus, per hunc in invisibilium amorem rapiamur."*

[84] St. Augustine, *Sermon 169* (sometimes known as *Sermon 15*): *"De verbis Apostoli."*

shall be saved, but he who does not believe shall be condemned."[85]

We take upon ourselves a frightful guilt when we fail to respond to Christian Revelation and to God's epiphany in Jesus. That we are responsible for our lack of faith proves that faith is not a pure gift from God, like some charismatic grace. The fact, moreover, that we are obligated to pray for an increase in faith again proves the necessary link between our faith and our own free will. To the extent, therefore, that our faith is lively, strong, and unshakable, we will accept the true and valid blissful aspect of death as a blessed union with Jesus.

Ways to increase our faith in God

The link between our faith and our free cooperation with God's grace is a mystery. Once again we touch here the *coincidence of opposites* which I have mentioned several times previously. On the one hand, faith is a pure gift, something we could never give to ourselves. On the other hand, it is also a free response on our part. These two facts are mysteriously intertwined. Beyond all doubt, faith is both a gift and a free response.

It remains a great mystery, however, how these two essential elements of faith, which at first glance seem contradictory, come together in the one reality of our faith. For our present purpose, it suffices that we realize that we must utter constant prayers for an increase in faith and thus achieve the full cooperation on our part for a faith which continues to grow and to become ever more firm and unshakable. Only in this way can

[85] Mark 16:16.

we be truly convinced of the blissful aspect of death as revealed in the words, "Behold, the Bridegroom cometh!"[86]

The framework of this present book does not permit a detailed analysis of the urgent necessity which men have to cooperate freely with the gift of faith. I can mention here only a few basic points.

We must, above all, protect our faith from all temptations to doubt. From the lives of many saints, of course, we learn that God often inflicted on them severe tests of faith. But our concern here is with those "tests" which we can blame on ourselves alone. Thus, thanks to a presumptuous evaluation of our own strength, we may read books hostile to faith, books that turn us away from Christ and the true Faith. To counter such dangers, we must cherish and preserve our faith as a precious gift from God; and in all humility we must be aware of our weaknesses.

Moreover, we must accord to inner prayer an important place in our life. Turning in a contemplative way toward Jesus, we must enter the depths of our soul and unite ourselves with Jesus in a reverent, loving way. This means that we must seek to be unencumbered, that we must turn away from the things surrounding us so as to concentrate on the absolute reality of God. When we become silent, when we let God speak, we can strengthen our faith. We open ourselves more and more to the experience of being drawn to the Father.[87]

Spiritual reading, too, provides helpful nourishment for the soul and for the growth of faith. Some word of Christ, some saying of an Apostle or a Church father, can suddenly light up

[86] Mt. 25:6.
[87] Cf. John 6:44.

a particular moment in the life of a saint. And how much this can contribute to an increase in our faith!

Finally, we must open ourselves to grasp God's message which is given through all the great natural benefits which come to us. We must let ourselves be led by the beauty of nature and art into God's presence, so that we see all things *in conspectu Dei* — in the framework of His existence and presence and light. We must allow ourselves, as it were, to walk along the inner path that leads also from all moral values to God. Again, we must heed the message God gives us in the deep happiness of loving and being loved, the happiness of a deep mutual affection. We must insert our earthly loves into the framework of God; we must love our neighbors "in God."[88] We must strive to "renew all things in Christ."[89] These are all decisions based on our own free will and they, too, are a way for us to grow in faith.

Faith transfigures death, but is also important in itself

To the extent, then, that faith is the axis of our life, is strong, alive, and deeply personal, the glorious aspect of death will triumph in us over the fearful and anxious aspect. But we must not misinterpret this truth as saying that a strong and unshakable faith is to be valued simply as a means to ensure the triumph of the glorious aspect. Quite apart from its altering greatly the aspect of death from dreadful fear to glorious and blissful union with the Bridegroom, faith in itself brings us something of immense value. Faith as such is incomparably more important and infinitely more valuable than its being

---

[88] Cf. the "*amare in Deo*" of St. Augustine, *Confessions*, 4.9.

[89] Cf. the "*instaurare omnia in Christo*" of Pope St. Pius X, from Eph. 1:10.

merely a means to let us see death in a supernatural light — as wondrous and as beneficial as this is. Faith is our principal response to God and to divine Revelation, to Jesus and to God's epiphany in Him, to eternal and absolute Truth. The glorious, supernatural view of death is only a fruit of faith, never a motive.

We ought to have faith because by our belief in God we give the response to which He is entitled. We ought to believe in divine Revelation because it is absolute truth. Just because the supernatural view is true, it must victoriously replace the natural aspect. Its absolute, supernatural truth must illuminate the great mystery of death and dispel the natural shadows.

Nothing would be more absurd than for us to regard the subjective happiness that results from the supernatural view of death as an end, and to see faith as a means for obtaining this end. To do so would mean detaching from truth both faith and the supernatural view of death. Such a pragmatic interpretation of faith comes close to a total misunderstanding of it. We must, therefore, condemn as blind nonsense the idea that, because it cheers and comforts us, a supernatural view of death is worth nourishing even if it is an illusion. Faith gives comfort only if it is true.

Love of Jesus also transforms our view of death

The dominance of the supernatural aspect of death in our souls depends not only on the degree of our faith but also on the degree of our love for Jesus, and for the Father in and through Jesus. Here, too, important gradations are to be found, from the upward glance of reverence all the way to a love filled with ardor and longing. Only when our love for Jesus becomes intense and our longing for union with Him becomes the very center of our lives (surpassing all other kinds of longing, yearning, desiring, or hoping) can the supernatural view of death victoriously eclipse the natural view. Only then can it triumph over the dread and pain of our being forced to depart from all the great goods that have given us happiness on earth — particularly our ardent communion with beloved persons, and above all, with the person we love most. Death's aspect is altered for us to the degree that we love Jesus and impatiently long to see Him face to face. A greater love for Him, a deeper and more unencumbered love, a stronger and more impetuous longing for complete union: such will change the face of death from dread to blissful fulfillment.

The natural aspect of death includes such fearful elements as the dreadful wasting away of the body, the disappearance of the entire reality around us, and the transition into a completely unknown situation. But all these things fade into the background against our longed-for, blissful union with the infinitely Holy One, the source of our joy, the Person loved more than anyone else. To the extent that our love for Jesus is unconditioned, limitless, and impatient, death's fearful aspect fades into the background — but it does not totally disappear.

Death's natural horrors must never be underestimated

We here touch on a general law of our personal existence on earth. In all matters, the natural aspect of something must never be ignored, but must rather be given its full weight and then eclipsed by the supernatural aspect. This means, for example, that we should not consider earthly suffering to be a beneficial good because it allows us to bear a cross joyfully with Christ and for His sake. Suffering should not be esteemed a replacement for things which naturally bring joy and also not for beneficial supernatural gifts such as charismatic graces. The character of the Cross *as cross* should not be eliminated from Christian life. Certainly we can endure joyfully a physical suffering for the sake of Christ, but the suffering does not thereby cease to cause pain; it is not changed into a sense of physical well-being.

There is a constant temptation here. We are human. Our transformation in Christ should not mean that we somehow cease to be human. The purely human, natural aspects of life must be faced and experienced even as we must transcend and outgrow them. We give a woefully incomplete response to the death of a beloved person, therefore, if we only rejoice; it may be that the dead person was like a saint and thus may confidently be expected to be enjoying eternal bliss. Even so, the human heart cries out with Virgil, "Here, tears are called for!"

When a beloved person dies, joy is an inappropriate response, in which we err in several respects. First, we ignore the reality of our frightful separation from her, our being robbed of her presence in this life. Second, we ignore the misfortune that death represents for the dead person herself. Related to this, we sometimes hear of persons who rejoice on being told that they will soon die of their lingering illness. Such persons run the risk of becoming giddy enthusiasts. They act as if death were not a great misfortune on the natural plane — as if death did not represent a form of punishment. They come dangerously close to ignoring the proper fear of the judgment.

The proper attitude toward death

The correct attitude toward death, I repeat, is otherwise. We must experience, we must pass through, all the fearful elements rooted in the natural view of death. For death is a punishment; it brings us to the judgment; it involves a fearful separation. It is hollow to short-circuit these things and to go immediately to the blissful aspect of death reflected in the phrase, "Behold, the Bridegroom cometh!"[90] Although the yearning for a blissful union with Jesus is sublime in itself, its reality must appear only at the end of a complete and authentic progression. Tears must come first.

Many pietistic poems and verses tend to ignore the natural aspects of death and to speak at once of the joys of eternity, with the inevitable result that such joys ring hollow and lack full reality. I think of such exclamations as, "O beloved hour, ring out the end of life!" or "I am disgusted at still being alive!" Bach set these verses to music which is far more serious and full of life's real resonances than are the words themselves. How far superior are these lines from the *Stabat Mater*[91]:

> *Quando corpus morietur,*
> *Fac, ut animae donetur*
> *Paradisi gloria.*

> While my body here decays,
> May my soul your goodness praise,
> Safe in your eternity.

In my book *Liturgy and Personality*, I analyzed the virtue of *discretio* and showed the necessity of our passing through certain stages in our relationship to other persons.[92] Something similar

---

[90] Mt. 25:6.

[91] *Sequence* for the votive *Mass of the Seven Sorrows of the Blessed Virgin Mary*, a composition by Jacapone da Todi.

[92] *Liturgy and Personality* (Manchester, NH: Sophia Institute Press, 1986), 115-138.

is at stake here in this question of the natural and supernatural aspects of death. We require a response to the total reality of death. The existential completeness of our response demands that we give to human tears the full weight of their sorrow before the eternal bliss of union with Jesus is allowed to dry them.

In summary, then, I say that the authentic attitude toward death — the God-intended attitude — is one which takes into account *all* the aspects of death according to an inner order of precedence. It is also one in which the blissful, supernatural aspect has the final triumphant word.

The supernatural view reveals the hierarchy of values

As we have already seen, the true hierarchy of all things shows up clearly when we recognize our life as a pilgrimage and when we go through this earthly life turned in hope toward our destination. Thus, far from making earthly life less significant, our having a supernatural view of death makes it far more significant. Let us consider this in greater detail.

The supernatural view will effect changes in our estimation of things. Many take on greater significance; others, far less significance. In the light of eternity, our conduct becomes in many ways more meaningful. Much that had at one time engaged our attention or disturbed us now becomes less important. We might say that the true order of importance of things — the real hierarchy of being — becomes more clearly etched for us in the light of eternity; in fact, only in this light is the true hierarchy evident.

I do not speak here of the hierarchy of values in general, as if only in the light of eternity are we able to know that Beethoven's *Ninth Symphony* is superior to his *First*, or that murder is a far greater moral evil than theft. My meaning here goes in a different direction: in the light of eternity, we come to understand that our first indispensable task in this life, our highest obligation, is that *we not offend God*. According to the words of Christ, love of God ranks first of the two commandments upon which the whole Law and the prophets depend.[93] This love is manifested especially in our giving no offense to God.

The *one thing necessary* (which Christ pointed out to the busy Martha) clearly is seen in the light of eternity to be our love of God.[94] And this implies, first, that we not offend Him by sin and then that we direct toward Him all the other manifestations of our love (which necessarily include our love of neighbor).

St. John of the Cross affirms that we shall be judged according to the degree of our love. He thus indicates the hierarchy we must ever keep in mind. All things related to the moral commandments enjoy an implicit superiority of rank, as well as a quite different importance, over all other achievements of whatever greatness and value. Compared to our moral rectitude, to our freedom from sin and our love of God, how truly unimportant and transient are so many of the things that engage us here so mightily! We think far too much of professional rank, reputation, and financial prosperity.

On the other hand, the light of eternity in no way diminishes the significance of really important earthly goods, such as the fate of persons close to us, above all those to whom we are bound by a special kind of love. What God wants of us in a particular situation gains significance through our expectation

[93] Matt. 22:36-40.
[94] Luke 10:38-42.

of eternity and our longing for eternal union with Jesus, and with the Father in and through Him. Moreover, the light of eternity increases the significance of small proofs of love and concern for others, even as it shows how everything worldly is relatively unimportant.

Only when we think of death — and of earthly life — in the supernatural light of eternity can we see the true rank of things. Only then can we appreciate the relatively trivial importance of so many things which, although they are morally legitimate, possess no real value but belong instead to the sphere of the merely agreeable.

The supernatural view increases gratitude for God's gifts

Moreover, I must emphasize that there are many gifts of God which, through their value, are a source of happiness for us on this earth, and for which deep gratitude is the proper response. Among these we could mention the recognition of profound truths, the enjoyment of beauty in nature and art, and, above all, our deep, loving communion with other humans — in friendship, marriage, or in family relationships with parents, brothers, and sisters. We should fully appreciate all these benefits.

Gratitude is one of the fundamental responses owed to God. Indeed, it includes appreciation of these good gifts which God has showered upon us as well as our enjoyment of these gifts and our grateful recognition of their role in our happiness. The light of eternity makes us all the more aware of these gifts which have graced our pilgrimage.

Our impetuous and impatient yearning and love for Jesus can only enhance our grateful appreciation for His loving kindness in granting us such good things.

Death's approach calls us to eternal concerns

There is need now to distinguish between two situations in our earthly life which call for different responses on our part. I refer to all those times when we are in relatively good health, able to discharge our normal duties, and to those other times when a serious illness, possibly fatal, overtakes us.

When relative health prevails, we must face the day-to-day tasks that are involved in our work and normal duties. They are then our theme. We are forced to focus our attention on all the details of daily life, no matter how much the supernatural view of death dominates our soul, no matter how our hearts long for eternity. To be sure, we must see all these daily tasks in their relation to eternity; we must shift worldly concerns to the background. In the spirit of St. Paul's advice, we "have no anxiety."[95] Nonetheless, attention to daily tasks is a part of the business at hand.

The focus changes, however, when we are felled by a serious illness which threatens to be fatal. Our focus now is on dying. Tasks that had hitherto engaged our attention have less importance in our eyes. Into the foreground of our consciousness comes the need to prepare for a good death, to assume in "the hour of our death"[96] an attitude that accords with God's wishes.

This total orientation toward eternity does not, however, involve a turning away from those we love. Quite the contrary! Just as the pain remains of our imminent separation from them, so, too, our love for them should take on a special kind of glow. Our closeness to eternity raises everything up to a solemn majesty. The light of eternity makes our heart more aware of

[95] Phil. 4:6.
[96] Conclusion of the *Hail Mary*.

those we love, more tenderly conscious of how much we love them. Even as our heart overflows with love for the Bridegroom — so soon to come! — our love for particular persons comes into even fuller bloom. At death's approach, everything non-essential fades away. Everything else becomes truer, more valid, and conclusive.

Faith and hope help us attain the supernatural view

As we have seen, God invites us — and *wills* us — to move past the natural, naive view of death and to embrace the supernatural view implicit in the expression, "Behold, the Bridegroom cometh!" Our acceptance of this invitation makes a significant difference for our earthly happiness. It also has great value in itself, since it is in agreement with revealed truth. It is, moreover, the fruit of our complete and profound living faith and of our ardent love for Jesus. This blissful supernatural view of death, therefore, belongs essentially to our transformation in Christ.

I have noted, however, that achieving the supernatural view is not entirely under our control. Neither is faith itself nor ardent love for Jesus. Each of these is in the first place a *gift*, something beyond our freedom to obtain. But each also demands a fundamental cooperation on our part. I mean now to analyze the role of our free cooperation in our gaining and deepening the supernatural view of death.

Our hope, which here on earth is directed toward eternal bliss, will vary according to the intensity of our faith and our love for God. The greater and more comprehensive our faith, the more impatient and ardent our love, the greater will be our supernatural hope. This hope presupposes faith in the continued existence of our soul.

True enough, we can be certain of our immortality through natural reason. But faith teaches us in quite a different way. By faith we know not only that the soul shall continue to exist, but also that through death we will attain our final and permanent way of existence. In faith we have responded to Revelation which tells us about the great alternative that awaits us after death: eternal damnation or eternal bliss (whether immediately after death or after a stay in Purgatory).

Faith, moreover, responds to the revelation of God's infinite mercy, as expressed in Jesus' words on the Cross to the repentant thief: "Amen I say to thee, this day thou shalt be with me in Paradise."[97] The same truth about God's mercy underlies the verse in the *Dies Irae* which pleads: "*Salva me, fons pietatis!*" ("Save me! O fount of mercy!")

The infinite mercy of God, therefore, is something revealed to us, along with the sobering truth that "It is a fearful thing to fall into the hands of the living God."[98] Through faith we know of God's mercy. This knowledge through faith is the very foundation of our hope of eternal bliss. But love also has a relation to hope. Our impetuous love for Jesus and our ardent desire for union with Him in a blissful, eternal present — this gives hope a central place in a highly meaningful way that is still quite different from faith. We may say that faith strengthens hope while love nourishes it.

Hope has two basic elements. The first is concerned with attaining a goal and thus is very similar to expectation. The second element deals with the positive value of the thing hoped for, the happiness for us which is related to the object of our hope. We may have expectation of some misfortune, but we

[97] Luke 23:43.
[98] Heb. 10:31.

never hope for it. Hope thus has something in common with mere wishing, since what it expects is always something good and beneficial.[99] But what chiefly determines the character of supernatural hope is that it absolutely counts on the intervention of Providence. Such hope allows us to regard death as a transition to eternal bliss and not to eternal damnation. All the while we are conscious of the fact that this bliss is the gift of God's mercy.

The supernatural view eliminates temptations to suicide

The Christian view of death includes our full understanding of the morally-required response to God. The supernatural view of death as the hour of judgment links it in a unique way with the question of moral good and evil. We cannot separate our being answerable to God from our moral conduct on earth. Nor can we separate the awareness of our responsibility from our faith in God as an absolute and righteous judge.

Our faith, therefore, has a clear understanding of the dreadful sin of suicide. Suicide loses all the attractive plausibility which it might have had when considered from the naive view of death. It is extremely important that we grasp how the supernatural view of death and of judgment before the personal God radically changes the natural view of suicide. For, notwithstanding our hope in God's mercy, our holy fear of the judgment includes a lively awareness of the sinfulness of suicide.

Besides the judgment, the supernatural view of death stresses also that death is the beginning of our eternal blissful union with Jesus. Suicide from this point of view, too, is understood as

[99] Cf. Appendices B and C.

a serious sin and an offense against God. It stands in absolute contradiction to our eternal union with the One who said: "You are my friends if you do the things I command you."[100]

Various steps are necessary for each of us to overcome the natural view of death and to replace it with the Christian perspective, which must include, as I have already stressed, a clear awareness of the sinfulness of suicide. This is particularly urgent for those who, by reason of their natural temperament, are especially tempted to suicide. They need to be made conscious of the fact that if they are stained with the sin of suicide, they cannot be justified in the sight of God and, indeed, that they will be excluded from eternal bliss. They must grasp the fact that suicide actually thwarts the healing of their sorrow and, in truth, makes it impossible for them to attain the goal they are seeking.

This is above all true of one who suffers a profound sorrow over the death of a beloved person. The longing for death here is highly intelligible and, in a sense, justified. But suicide as a way of solving the emptiness and longing is senseless. Those who long for death and see it as an easy way out of sorrows and troubles, must somehow come to see that suicide is a totally unsuitable way of escape. How could a fearful sin possibly help us escape from the dreadful sorrows of this life into a better place in which our tears are wiped away? The truly liberating character of death excludes all suicide, whether direct or indirect. What is uniquely frightful about the sin of suicide is that it is committed at the instant of the conclusion of life, with hardly the possibility of contrition which all other kinds of sins have.

[100]John 15:14.

Through suicide we close off the way to the very place we desire, where tears and sorrows vanish.[101]

As Christians, moreover, our longing for eternal union with Jesus necessarily includes the awareness that we belong to Christ and not to ourselves.

We must always be mindful of the truth that the question of our eternal bliss will be decided by our conduct in this life, and that our transformation in Christ has to be accomplished here on earth. Suicide is incompatible with our transformation in Christ, therefore, not only because it is a sin but also because our arbitrary termination of our own life destroys the possibility of our glorifying God through the full interval of time He has designated as the length of our pilgrimage. Suicide robs us of the chance to work for our own transformation.

Finally, those persons contemplating suicide should recognize that earth is not just a valley of tears. As the Liturgy says of Creation, "The heavens and the earth are filled with Thy glory, O God!" Such persons need to understand how indispensable is gratitude for the correct response to God. Gratitude is a prerequisite for our eternal bliss; it necessarily forms part of all those earthly gifts that are included in our transformation in Christ.

We must pray now for a death pleasing to God

Our constant prayer for growth in faith, hope, and love contains implicitly a prayer that we may die in a way pleasing to God. It contains also the request that the supernatural view

---

[101]This is true, of course, only in the case of a suicide carried out in a free and cold-blooded manner. It is not valid, however, for the countless cases in which, for example, suicide is a consequence of a nervous breakdown or mental disease. In such cases, sinfulness is diminished or entirely absent. — Ed.

of death may gain victory in our consciousness, so that we may see death as the gate to an eternal, blissful union with Jesus and with the Holy Trinity in and through Jesus.

Holy sobriety, which is also a basic component of holiness, reminds us of certain serious dangers and temptations which may befall us concerning death. Death may come suddenly and unexpectedly. Or else our spirit may become weakened after a long illness, so that we find ourselves unable to pray in full alertness, unable to throw ourselves into the arms of the merciful God.

Holy sobriety teaches us to use wisely the times of our physical health. While we are still able, we must concentrate our thoughts on eternity. We must fully experience remorse for all our sins while, at the same time, we implore God's pardon and mercy.[102]

---

[102]We must also never forget how swiftly the possibility for prayer or remorse may cease: we might suffer a fatal heart attack or die in our sleep. I have myself experienced in an instant the fading away of my life's strength and even my consciousness because of a serious circulatory problem. Such things can happen so quickly that we have not even the time to call upon Jesus in a final, hasty prayer. Only a second marks the transition from full consciousness and well-being to the night of unconsciousness. There is not even time to think about what is happening. We experience only the swift disappearance of all our vital signs.

XVI

Death and the ultimate fulfillment of love

LET us suppose now that God has granted us the grace of seeing death primarily as the gateway to our eternal blissful union with Jesus, without, however, ignoring all the other aspects. There still remains for us the painful farewell we must bid to persons we deeply love — above all, to the one we love most of all.

Our love for the human persons whom God has given us in a special way continues to exist. It in no way diminishes as our love for Jesus increases, deepens, and becomes more ardent. On the contrary, the greater our love for Jesus, the more deeply are we able to love others in the genuine way that St. Augustine stressed when he spoke of *loving others in God*.[103]

---

[103]St. Augustine, *Confessions*, 4.9. It should be noted that our special *love for individual persons* is not the same as *love of neighbor*. This latter love, in its true Christian sense, is an immediate consequence of our love for Jesus. It is charity — *caritas* — and cannot exist apart from our love for Jesus. Appendix D considers this difference in greater detail. See also Chap. 11 of my book, *Das Wesen der Liebe*, vol. 3 of *Gesammelte Werke* (Regensburg: Habbel, 1971).

No love we have for any human person is irreconcilable with the unconditional love of our hearts for Jesus. No matter what kind of love is at stake (spousal, parental, filial, or the love proper to friendship) and no matter how great and deep is the love we have for human persons, so long as it is a love *in God* and not *outside of God*, it can grow and intensify along with our love for Jesus. Jesus, therefore, is not the rival or the competitor of beloved human persons.

Our great love for another person, if it is not an *amare in Deo* — that is, a love consciously and expressly embedded in our love of Jesus — *can* hinder our absolute devotion to Jesus. This happens when Jesus does not rule our relationship and the harmony of love we feel for each other is not rooted in Jesus. But even here, differences exist. Thus, the passionate response of a love borne only of human impulses is a greater hindrance than a response that maintains a noble spirituality amidst its ardor and that is sanctioned by the inner fiber of our being. But if even this latter kind of love fails to be an *amare in Deo*, it, too, in its own way will be a hindrance. The intense love we have for a person who preoccupies us totally is, then, a rival to our absolute devotion to Jesus — and a grave hindrance.

The more we love Jesus, the greater and deeper is our love for specific persons. This latter love, although it is filled with *caritas*, loses none of its own particular character. Far from devaluing or minimizing our love for human persons, our love of Jesus causes these human loves to be even more themselves, even more brightly and deeply formed.

Love for particular persons must be anchored in Jesus

I ask again the question which I posed before: given that death serves as a transition to our blissful union with Jesus, does not death yet continue to be something painful and distressing because it separates us from our loved ones, above all, from the one we love most? Will not our death bring about a twofold sorrow: our own suffering over being separated from those whom we love, and their great sorrow over losing us, even if only for a short time?

Yes, death continues to be painful and should remain so. But the deep sorrow of all concerned is transfigured through the light of Christ. A new dimension in our human relationship mysteriously emerges alongside the sorry realities of death (the disappearance of the dead person and the radical, although only temporary, rupture of our communion of love). Let us see why this is so.

All humans — and thus all those to whom we are especially tied by a great love — are associated in a profound way with Jesus Christ. The very *raison d'être* for humans is precisely their achievement of the Beatific Vision and their union with Jesus, and "in Him, through Him, and with Him," with the Father and the Holy Spirit.

In various places[104] I have already pointed out that any deep human love, and most especially the exclusive love of married couples, must be anchored in Jesus if it is to be truly and fully itself. Any deep love not so anchored has come to a standstill.

Love has two innermost tendencies or intentions: *union* and *benevolence*, which can almost be spoken of as the genius of love. These can develop fully only when the lovers meet each other in Christ, only when their love is anchored in Jesus.[105]

[104]Dietrich von Hildebrand, *Marriage* (Manchester, NH: Sophia Institute Press, 1984); *Das Wesen der Liebe*, vol. 3 of *Gesammelte Werke* (Regensburg: Habbel, 1971), 293, 326 ff.
[105]*Das Wesen der Liebe*, 335, 350 ff.

The profoundest love union is possible only in Jesus

The *intention of union* falls short of its complete goal unless
it reaches into that deepest chamber of the loved one's soul to
which Christ alone has the key. Each soul's relationship to Jesus
resides in this most central and important chamber, this incomparably profound place in each human heart. For those who
have not found Christ and who do not love Him reverently as
the God-Man, this chamber remains empty. If we love such
persons, we can never penetrate into this deepest region; we
cannot achieve the deepest possible union with them. Despite
all our longing for perfect union, we remain on the threshold of
our beloved.

If, however, our beloved has found Jesus, then the eternally
beloved Bridegroom of my soul dwells in her inmost soul, too.
Our love can then be anchored in Jesus, and the ardent yearning we feel for deepest union with each other can now be
realized — in Jesus, and in nothing else.

Only Jesus can give our beloved ultimate happiness

This applies analogously also to the *intention of benevolence*,
whereby we desire the greatest happiness for our beloved and
we wish to provide her all good things. In our loving embrace
of her total being, an outspoken *affirmation* of her is included.
But this is possible only if we understand that she has been
created *for* Jesus and belongs *to* Him.

Only Jesus can bestow ultimate happiness on her and, what
is more, eternal bliss. Every deep love anchored in Jesus necessarily includes, moreover, an inner gesture that would blissfully
fulfill this *being ordered toward God* of each of the lovers. The
lovers participate in this mysterious solidarity in a way that far

exceeds mere knowledge, for it is accomplished in Jesus. This is the highest fulfillment of love's intention of benevolence, of our burning desire to see eternal bliss as the lot of our precious beloved. It is also a blissful participation on our part in the deepest meaning of her mysterious existence. We experience this mutual achievement also as part of the high point of our *intention of union*, indeed as the final fulfillment of our love for her.

Thus, all the lines of life converge in Jesus, who is the king and center of all hearts. This fact consoles us when we must face sad absences and, especially, the cruel separation of death. This fact also plays a key role in every earthly love of ours which is anchored in Jesus.

In my book on love, I show how one important dimension of every love is the "face-to-face" mutual glance of love — the *I-Thou* relation between the partners.[106] This glance will in no way be diminished when my love for another is anchored in Jesus.

Love yearns for the beloved's perfect union with Jesus

My participation in her *being ordered toward God* does not negate or conceal our mutual surrender to each other. Direct unity in Jesus would never be perfect if my beloved's participation in the final association with Jesus and love of Him were not proposed. From its significance in and of itself, the unity of convergence belongs also to the perfect direct unity of love in Jesus — as a participation in the most profound theme of my

[106]*Das Wesen der Liebe*, chap. 6, esp. 173 ff.; 179 ff.

loved one and in spite of the deep, formal difference existing between unity of convergence and direct unity.

We deal here with two different dimensions of love. In the one, we exchange mutual glances of love in Jesus. In the other — impelled by love — I participate in the *being ordered toward God* of my beloved and she reciprocates by participating in my own *being ordered toward God*. We are thus united in an ultimate convergence — of interests, welfare, and destiny. Each shares with the other the perfect fulfillment of each one's destiny: the loving union with Jesus and, through Him, with the Father and the Holy Spirit.

Even so, I must emphasize again that this union rooted in convergence in no way conceals or erases the mutual *frontal glance* — the *I-thou* relation — of the lovers who love each other in Christ. In fact, the unity of convergence belongs also to the perfect frontal union in Jesus. The latter would never be perfect if it lacked my participation in my beloved's ultimate *being ordered toward God*. The unity of convergence, therefore, has a double importance: in itself it represents my participation in the deepest theme of my beloved. Second, it forms part of the perfect *I-thou* unity of love in Jesus.

In a certain way, of course, my participation in the *being ordered toward God* of my beloved represents the crowning achievement of love, the last word of love, the final statement which I direct toward her. For this is the ultimate theme of her existence: something, moreover, willed by God and accomplished in and through Jesus. I am united with her in her destiny. And — great gift of God! — the convergence is reciprocated: she unites with me in the achievement of my ultimate goal. This union is unique because it has to do with the most valid, most profound, and most characteristic reality, i.e., the question of the vocation and destiny of man, the original theme of humanity. This theme begins, indeed, on the natural plane but then goes far beyond into unapproachable and mysterious heights. St. Augustine says of the Beatific Vision: "*Ibi vacabimus et videbimus; videbimus et amabimus; amabimus et laudabimus. Ecce quod erit in fine sine fine.*" ("There we shall rest and see, see and love, love and praise. This is what shall be in the end without end.")[107]

This vision is simultaneously the most intimate and private and also the most open of all things (in the sense of a *holy openness*). It means first of all the most profound union between God and the individual soul, immersed, as it were, in secret and intimate delights. But it also signifies that which we ultimately have most in common with all other persons. It is thus the culmination both of our union with Jesus, in which everything else fades away, and of our most profound communion with all other persons. With respect to this latter, however, we must note that our oneness with those we love — above all, with the one we love most of all — is again something distinct and unique. "*Quanto notiores, tanto cariores,*" says St. Augustine: "The better they are known, the dearer they become."[108]

As I have stressed above, my beloved and I are joined in looking at Jesus and rejoicing in Him in a way that does not cancel the direct and mutual glance of love between us. This rejoicing in unison is rather the culmination of our mutual love. The *thou* which each of us is to the other is not set aside; rather a sublime *we* is born out of the most profound *I-thou* relationship, fulfilling and completing the deepest theme of love.

---

[107]*The City of God*, 22.30, trans. Marcus Dods, vol. 18 of *The Great Books of the Western World* (Chicago: Encyclopedia Britannica, 1952).

[108]St. Augustine, *Epistola*, 92.1.

As a result, when the hour of death strikes for one of us and we accomplish the decisive face-to-face meeting with Jesus in the communion of love which is the destiny and goal of us all, a truly new dimension of communion with our beloved is actualized. The sorrows of death, illuminated now by the ultimate reality of eternal light, are transfigured.

"Behold, the Bridegroom cometh!"

The Christian view of death is wonderfully expressed by the words: "Behold, the Bridegroom cometh! Go forth to meet Him!"[109] We must attend now to what the last few words mean. Here we are at the hour of death, at the very moment of death. All our faculties fade and disappear.

Then the words are heard, summoning us to a spontaneous act of cooperation: our meeting with Jesus. What a wonderful, mysterious hurrying is urged on our soul — to hasten toward our Redeemer, our Bridegroom, our Lover! Here, indeed, is a victory over the dreadful natural aspect of death and a victory that we ourselves experience. The Christian view of death stands forth in all its glory, the fruit of a strong and deep faith, of an ardent, yearning, and impatient love, and a hope that is now victorious.

Our love for Jesus includes many different stages. We start with a reverent kind of love which wills to follow Jesus, animated by His words: "You are my friends if you do the things I command you."[110] And it ends with the ardent surrender of our hearts to Jesus in a most intimate relationship: "My heart hath

[109]Mt. 25:6.
[110]John 15:14.

said to Thee, I have sought Thy face! Thy face, O Lord, I will seek: turn not away Thy face from me!"[111]

These heartfelt words express the high point of the *intention of union*. Our yearning for Jesus springs from a personal, intimate, ardent and profound love. It moves us to utter the following prayer:

> *In hora mortis meae voca me.*
> *Et jube me venire ad te,*
> *Ut cum sanctis tuis laudem te*
> *In saecula saeculorum.*[112]

> In the hour of my death call me
> And bid me come to Thee,
> That with the saints, I may praise Thee
> For ever and ever! Amen.

Let us note the ardor and impatience in the request, "Bid me come to Thee!" Such overflowing and impatient love is the very soul of the glorious Christian view of death, causing our hearts to tremble in jubilation at the words: "Behold, the Bridegroom cometh! Go forth to meet Him!"

[111]*Introit* of the Mass for the Sunday after the Ascension: *"Tibi dixit cor meum, quaesivi vultum tuum; vultum tuum, Domine, requiram: ne avertas faciem tuam a me."* (Cf. Ps. 26:8.)

[112]Conclusion of the medieval prayer, *Anima Christi*.

Biographical Note
Dietrich von Hildebrand (1889-1977)

HITLER feared him and Pope Pius XII called him "the twentieth century Doctor of the Church." For more than six decades, Dietrich von Hildebrand — philosopher, spiritual writer, and anti-Nazi crusader — led philosophical, religious, and political groups, lectured throughout Europe and the Americas, and published more than thirty books and many more articles. His influence was widespread and endures to this day.

Although he was a deep and original thinker on subjects ranging across the spectrum of human interests, nonetheless, in his lectures and in his writings, von Hildebrand instinctively avoided extravagant speculations and convoluted theories. Instead, he sought to illuminate the nature and significance of seemingly "everyday" elements of human existence that are easily misunderstood and too frequently taken for granted.

Therefore, much of von Hildebrand's philosophy concerns the human person, the person's interior ethical and affective life, and the relations that should exist between the person and the world in which he finds himself.

Jaws of Death: Gate of Heaven

Von Hildebrand's background made him uniquely qualified to examine these topics. He was born in beautiful Florence in 1889, the son of the renowned German sculptor, Adolf von Hildebrand. At the time, the von Hildebrand home was a center of art and culture, visited by the greatest European artists and musicians of the day. Young Dietrich's early acquaintance with these vibrant, creative people intensified his natural zest for life.

In Florence, von Hildebrand was surrounded by beauty — the overwhelming natural beauty of the Florentine countryside and the rich beauty of the many art treasures that are Florence's Renaissance heritage. Pervading this Florentine atmosphere was Catholicism: in the art, in the architecture, and in the daily life of the people. These early years in Florence quickened in von Hildebrand a passionate love of truth, of goodness, of beauty, and of Christianity.

As he grew older, he developed a deep love for philosophy, studying under some of the greatest of the early twentieth century German philosophers, including Edmund Husserl, Max Scheler, and Adolf Reinach. Converting to Catholicism in 1914, von Hildebrand taught philosophy for many years at the University of Munich.

However, soon after the end of World War I, Nazism began to threaten von Hildebrand's beloved southern Germany. With his characteristic clearsightedness, von Hildebrand immediately discerned its intrinsic evil. From its earliest days, he vociferously denounced Nazism in articles and speeches throughout Germany and the rest of Europe.

Declaring himself unwilling to continue to live in a country ruled by a criminal, von Hildebrand regretfully left his native Germany for Austria, where he continued teaching philosophy (now at the University of Vienna) and fought the Nazis with even greater vigor, founding and editing a prominent anti-Nazi newspaper, *Christliche Ständestaat*.

This angered both Heinrich Himmler and Adolf Hitler, who were determined to silence von Hildebrand and to close his anti-Nazi newspaper. Orders were given to have von Hildebrand assassinated in Austria. However, von Hildebrand evaded the hit-squads and, thanks to his Swiss passport, was finally able to flee the country just as it fell to the Nazis.

It is characteristic of von Hildebrand that even while he was engaged in this dangerous life-and-death struggle against the Nazis, he maintained his deep spiritual life, and managed to write during this period his greatest work, the sublime and highly-acclaimed spiritual classic, *Transformation in Christ*.[113]

Fleeing from Austria, von Hildebrand was pursued through many countries, ultimately arriving on the shores of America in 1940 by way of France, Spain, Portugal, and Brazil.

Penniless in New York after his heroic struggle against the Nazis, von Hildebrand was hired as professor of philosophy at Fordham University where he taught until his retirement. Many of his best works were written during this period and after his retirement. He died in 1977 in New Rochelle, New York.

Dietrich von Hildebrand was remarkable for his keen intellect, his profound originality, his prodigious output, his great personal courage, his deep spirituality, and his intense love of truth, goodness, and beauty. These rare qualities made Dietrich von Hildebrand one of the greatest philosophers and one of the wisest men of the twentieth century.

---

[113]*Available from Sophia Institute Press*

Appendix A

Wagner's relation to Schopenhauer

WAGNER was a known admirer of Schopenhauer when he composed *Tristan and Isolde*. Some critics have insisted, therefore, that the aspect of death stressed in *Tristan and Isolde* is a *going down into nothingness*, into Nirvana, rather than a positive view which is based on the soul's continued existence in another and better life. The critics can quote in their favor the love/death scene of the final act, which concludes with these words:

> *Ertrinken —*
> *versinken —*
> *unbewußt —*
> *höchste Lust!*[114]

To respond to these critics, we must recall the more detailed description of the lovers' death wish which is given in act 2, sc. 2. It stands in sharp contradiction to the words just quoted, which end the opera. In this earlier scene, the lovers exclaim:

---

[114]"To drown,/ To sink,/ Unconscious,/ O highest bliss!" *Tristan and Isolde*, act 3, sc. 4.

139

Jaws of Death: Gate of Heaven

> *So starben wir,*
> *um ungetrennt,*
> *ewig einig,*
> *ohne End',*
> *ohn' Erwachen,*
> *ohn' Erbangen,*
> *namenlos*
> *in Lieb' umfangen,*
> *ganz uns selbst gegeben,*
> *der Liebe nur zu leben."*[115]

Obviously *"der Liebe nur zu leben"* ("to live for love alone") demands the fully conscious existence of the two persons after death. How then can we harmonize these stirring words in act 2 with the seeming reference to *going down into nothingness* which ends the opera?

The contradiction is explained when we consider that two very different things operate in the mind of any creative artist: the one is his artistic talent itself, the other is his view of life based on the influence of some philosopher. Often enough it happens that the talent of artists will carry their creative work far beyond their theoretical philosophy of life. Their artistic gifts will force them even to forget their theoretical philosophy and move their creative work into the world of truth. Precisely this happens in Part 1 of Goethe's *Faust*. When Gretchen asks Faust whether he is a Christian, he replies with a pantheistic creed that corresponds to Goethe's own philosophy of life.[116]

But all this is forgotten — and contradicted — at the end of Part 1. In the passage dealing with Gretchen's death, an angel voice from above proclaims that "she is saved!"[117] With these words Goethe sweeps away his pantheistic ideas and puts before our eyes the world of truth — the true Christian world. His play reveals that the objective truth of reality

---

[115]"Let us die then,/ Together,/ Eternally one and forever,/ With no awakening,/ With no trembling,/ Nameless and by love enveloped,/ May we surrender to one another/ And live for love alone!" *Tristan and Isolde*, act 2, sc. 2.

[116]*Faust*, pt. 1, lines 3418 ff.

[117]*Faust*, pt. 1, lines 4612 ff.

triumphs over his theoretical philosophy. His artistic talent forces him past his philosophy, forces him to give the final word to objective truth in its fully classical form.

So, too, with Wagner's *Tristan and Isolde*. Its ultimate theme is the love of a man and a woman, and the deepest metaphysical implications and consequences of such a love. Such a theme calls for the continued existence of the lovers' souls in another life. The ultimate fulfillment of the *intentio unionis* which death brings about, the blissful state of *living for love alone* — necessarily demands the continued existence of the individual soul beyond earthly death.

Hope, expectation, wishing, & desire

HOPE has much in common with *expectation*, but clearly differs from it because hope always presupposes God and His Providence, whereas expectation is based on purely natural prospects with no presuppositions about Providence. Hope, moreover, always involves an objective benefit for us, whereas expectation can also be concerned with neutral things or even with misfortunes about to happen to us.

In this aspect of dealing with something positive, therefore, hope resembles *desire*. But hope differs from desire precisely through what hope has in common with expectation: the theme of the intervention of some future happening. As we have seen, hope necessarily counts on an all-powerful, infinitely good God. For unbelievers and atheists, this objective presupposition of all hope exists only implicitly. They are not aware of God, but the very fact of their hoping proves that they carry this presupposition of God unknowingly in their hearts.

The very essence of hope demands that it be not exclusively a value-response. Hope must always include reference to an objective benefit for myself — some concern of mine is always in the foreground. In this respect, hope differs from pure value-responses such as admiration, enthusiasm, veneration, love, or adoration. Hope must always include something specifically of benefit to me, such as being spared a great misfortune to myself from some threat to me or a loved one. Again, hope is always directed toward something in the future that does not yet exist. This fact, too, distinguishes hope from responses like love and reverence.

In this respect, hope resembles *willing*, which is directed toward the future realization of a certain state of facts not yet existing. But hope is the very opposite of willing in a crucial respect: in hope we necessarily grasp that the realization of the desired state of facts emphatically does not lie within our own power. In willing, on the other hand, we explicitly intend that the future state of facts be realized through our own intervention. We say, as it were, to the future event: "You must come into being and, indeed, you must do so through my own activity."

Let us also note here that *wishing* is still different from willing. I no doubt always wish for the very thing I hope for; in many instances I also wish for the very thing I will to happen. But each of these three attitudes has its own identity, its own essential elements.

We may be tempted to believe that hoping and willing are ultimately the same, for the reason that hope accompanies all our willings. Christians are aware that they depend in all things upon God, that upon God depends the successful outcome of all the things which they can and should achieve through their own power.

But the fact that hope always accompanies willing does not erase their essential differences, their separate, inner meanings. A favorable outcome of my actions, which is the goal of hope, does not even lie within my own power. Even when I pledge to do all I can to achieve some result, the outcome is related to something that only God can grant. Thus I will to do something and I simultaneously hope that God will grant me a successful outcome — which outcome lies beyond my power.

As already noted, hope has as one of its attributes the element of expectation. Hope takes a position toward the real occurrence of some desired state of affairs and counts on the fact that this state of affairs will be achieved. In this sense, hope belongs more to the class of *theoretical responses* than to the class of *affective* responses.[118] Hope has an element of conviction. This fact clearly distinguishes hope from the mere wishing for something to happen.

---

[118]Cf. Dietrich von Hildebrand, *The Heart* (Chicago: Franciscan Herald Press, 1977).

Appendix C

The formal objects of hope

OUR hope can be directed toward all kinds of natural benefits, and these are subject to important gradations. But a new and still more decisive difference has to do with whether the formal object of our hope is an earthly benefit (of whatever gradation) or our eternal bliss. It is just this latter which is the concern of the truly *theological* virtue of hope. This strictly supernatural virtue is directed toward our eternal union with Jesus and — in Him and through Him — with God the Father in the Beatific Vision.

By way of contrast there is the hope which we can call *natural hope*, concerned with benefits that are natural and are objectively beneficial to us. To understand supernatural hope better (which, like faith and charity, is a theological virtue), we must briefly look at natural hope.

Natural hope, first of all, is something that can aim at objective benefits not only for ourselves but also for others. Thus we can hope that we ourselves shall recover from a certain grave illness but we can also hope that some other person shall recover. Her recovery will certainly be a great objective benefit for her, but if we love her (and precisely to the degree that we love her), her recovery is also a beneficial good.

In my book, *Das Wesen der Liebe*, I have shown that when it comes to those we love, we are concerned not only with the value-aspect of what they do or what they undergo, but also with their welfare *for their own sake.*[119] Love ordains that the good fortune of loved ones is a source of happiness for us, even as their misfortune is a source of sorrow for us.

Quite apart from this solidarity with our beloved in good or bad fortune, there is a further consideration. Not simply when I love someone with the love that is called Christian charity, but also in a personal love, it can happen that a misfortune for my beloved constitutes simultaneously a misfortune for me just because my beloved is a great source of joy to me. Thus, if she should be gravely ill, I sorrow in solidarity with her own sorrow over the threatened loss of her good health and even her life; but I sorrow also for my own imminent loss because the sickness threatens such a great source of my happiness.

It follows from the above that the *formal object* of our hope for the welfare of someone loved by us is a benefit for us, even when our hope is directed in the first place to the welfare itself of our beloved, e.g., that she recover from illness.

But are there not cases where the formal object of our hope is indeed associated with important values which yet are not objective benefits for ourselves? Would this not be true when we hope for the triumph of justice somewhere in the world? Or when we hope for the collapse of communism even if we shall no longer be alive to witness this happy event?

The successful realization of such hopes would indeed be an important happening in and of itself — a value — but it would also be an objective benefit for humanity. So, too, but in an incomparably higher way, our hope that the whole world will someday be converted to Christ and His Church has as its primary goal a pure value, namely, the glory of God. But the achieved goal will also be of the highest objective benefit to mankind, to all those men now converted to the truth.

We are thus correct in saying that the formal goal of hope always represents an outright objective benefit for both myself and others: in all cases when it is a benefit for others, it is also indirectly a benefit for me.

There is a further distinction which at least deserves mention here. Among the formal objects of hope, it is important to examine whether it is a value whose realization we hope for, or whether it is a beneficial good for us which is in the foreground.

---

[119]*Das Wesen der Liebe*, ch. 7.

Appendix D

Love of Jesus and love of neighbor

THE depth and fullness of our love of neighbor depends exclusively on our love for Jesus. Moreover, it necessarily flows from this love. Love of neighbor cannot be lacking when there is an unconditioned love of Jesus. It rather emerges necessarily from this love. Our love of neighbor requires no special relation on our part to our neighbor, nor any particular power to love. So long as we have the power to love Jesus, and to love Him in an unconditioned way, our love of neighbor is ensured.

Admittedly, different persons have different capacities for love. The greatest and ultimate surrender of one heart can be objectively less than that of someone else. But, whatever the capacity of an individual person, each increase in his love of Jesus necessarily means an increase in his love of neighbor.

The fact that our love of neighbor has a direct relation to our love for Jesus, so that the one varies directly with the other, finds no counterpart in our love for specific individual humans: a parent, a child, a friend, a fiancé, or a spouse. For these loves can exist without our having a total love for Jesus.

If our love is not an *amare in Deo*, it will indeed lack a final dimension of depth, but it can still be a great and ardent love. I am thinking here of examples taken from literature and from music: Orpheus and Euridice, Alcestis, and above all, Tristan and Isolde.

Jaws of Death: Gate of Heaven

These individual loves, moreover, always demand a personal affinity, a special *word* by God to the lovers. These loves do not necessarily flow from our love for Jesus, as does love of neighbor. In principle, therefore, it is possible that a man should love Jesus with the greatest fervor and devotion and still not have love for any other person, apart from love of neighbor. I say *in principle* because the lack of any natural love for another person is generally a sign of great emotional poverty.

Ordinarily, unconditioned love of Jesus goes hand in hand with the ability to love another person in some way or another. All of the saints displayed a great, radiant, and boundless love for Jesus, and, as a rule, they were also capable of feeling great love for others. Let us think, for example, of how St. Thérèse of Lisieux loved her father, how St. Augustine loved his mother and his son, Adeodatus, and how St. Elizabeth loved her husband.

The link between my love for Jesus and the consequent love for my neighbor differs in yet another respect from the link between my love for Jesus and my love for a particular person. The latter love presupposes a special affinity between my beloved and me. My love for Jesus cannot be a substitute for this affinity in any of my natural loves. It is essential, rather, that I meet someone who appeals to my heart in a special way and not simply *as a neighbor*. God's Providence is decisive here in putting me in contact with a person able to awaken love within my heart. He whose love for Jesus is ultimate need not have met a human person who has inflamed his heart with love and has reciprocated this love — but in human relationships, reciprocity plays a fundamental role.

SOPHIA INSTITUTE PRESS

Sophia Institute is a non-profit institution that seeks to restore man's knowledge of eternal truth, including man's knowlege of his own nature, his relation to other persons, and his relation to God.

Sophia Institute Press serves this end in a number of ways. It publishes translations of foreign works to make them accessible for the first time to English-speaking readers. It brings back into print many books that have long been out-of-print. And it publishes important new books that fulfill the ideals of Sophia Institute. These books afford readers a rich source of the enduring wisdom of mankind.

Sophia Institute Press makes high-quality books available to the general public by using advanced, cost-effective technology and by soliciting donations to subsidize general publishing costs. Your generosity can help us provide the public with editions of works containing the enduring wisdom of the ages. Send your tax-deductible contribution to the address noted below. Your questions, comments, and suggestions are also welcome.

For a free catalog, call:

Toll-Free: 1-800-888-9344

SOPHIA INSTITUTE PRESS
BOX 5284
MANCHESTER, NH 03108

Sophia Institute Press is a tax-exempt institution as defined by the Internal Revenue Service Code, Section 501(c)(3). Tax I.D. 22-2548708.